D1007907

# THE
# Cat
# Behavior
# ANSWER BOOK

ARDEN MOORE

ILLUSTRATED BY MATT AMBRE

FOREWORD BY NANCY PETERSON

Storey Publishing

*The mission of Storey Publishing is to serve our customers by
publishing practical information that encourages
personal independence in harmony with the environment.*

Edited by Lisa H. Hiley
Cover design and art direction by Mary Winkelman Velgos
Cover photo by Lynne and Marvin Carlton/2C imagery
Text design by Jessica Armstrong
Text production by Jennifer Jepson Smith
Illustrations © Matt Ambre
Indexed by Susan Olason, Indexes & Knowledge Maps

Printed in China by Regent Publishing Services
10 9 8 7 6 5 4 3

**Library of Congress Cataloging-in-Publication Data**

Moore, Arden.
    The cat behavior answer book : practical insights & proven
    solutions for your feline questions / Arden Moore ; illustrated
    by Matt Ambre ; foreword by Nancy Peterson.
        p. cm.
    Includes bibliographical references.
    ISBN 978-1-58017-674-3 (pbk. : alk. paper)
    1. Cats—Behavior—Miscellanea.  I. Title.
SF446.5.M63 2007
636.8—dc22
                                                        2007005183

# DEDICATION

I dedicate this book to my delightful friends Cindy
Benedict, Flo Frum, and Dr. Jill Richardson; my pet-
loving siblings Deb, Karen, and Kevin; my wonderful
niece Chrissy and nephew Andy; my felines Callie and
Murphy; and to the memory of Little Guy and my first
cool cat, Corky.

# CONTENTS

## PART I: Feeling Fine about Being Feline . . . . . . . . . . . . 1

Find out what makes a cat behave like a cat. Learn
about feline senses, emotions, and instincts. Discover
fascinating facts about cat intelligence, feral cats, and
different breeds.

## PART II: Chatting with Your Cat . . . . . . . . . . . . . . . . . . 61

Our cats often seem to be trying to tell us something,
if only we could figure it out. Learn about the power
of purring, unravel the mysteries of meows, and hone
your "cat chat" skills.

## PART III: Kitty Quirks and Funny Felines . . . . . . . . . 117

Our furry companions have many peculiar habits.
Find out what the deal is with chewing on plastic,
climbing the curtains, playing with water, and much
more. And what's the fuss about catnip, anyway?

# FOREWORD

Many of my childhood memories involve cats. I regularly rescued strays, but my mother insisted that I find them homes. I often practiced walking on all fours and lapping up milk from a bowl — a habit that no one has admitted sharing with me.

I finally got my first cat, Shasta, when I was an adult. Alas, my happiness was brief because my landlords insisted that Shasta depart. I mustered the courage to speak to them because, although I'd only had her for a few days, I was smitten. My landlords and their beagle hated cats, so I promised they would never see Shasta because she would be kept indoors. I begged them to let me keep her, and they finally agreed.

Two years later I prepared to move across country. My landlords asked if I was taking Shasta; they were afraid I would leave her in the apartment. The only thing I left in the apartment was a decrepit old chair. Its springs were protruding when I moved in, but now the chair was in shreds — evidence of my failure to provide a scratching post for Shasta.

I was 28 years old when Shasta and I arrived in California and 30 when I earned my credentials as a registered veterinary technician. I worked in a veterinary hospital for the next 12 years and brought home more cats. I also convinced my friends and family that their lives weren't complete without a feline friend.

Over the years, I've learned a lot about keeping cats healthy and caring for sick ones. I noticed that although veterinary clients and staff were likely to talk about annoying dog behaviors, discussions about cat behaviors were rarely part of the office visit. Cats have suffered as a result. They have been labeled as unfriendly, spiteful, mischievous, and worse. They have been abandoned, given away, brought to shelters, and euthanized, when all they have done was behave like cats.

I made many mistakes with my first cats because I just didn't know any better. I wish I'd had this book to help me prevent, manage, and understand my cats' behaviors. And although I'm much savvier today, Arden's book has taught this "old dog" some new tricks about cat behavior. Arden and her team of animal-behavior experts will educate and entertain you page after page. Start reading your way to the best relationship you can have with your cat!

— NANCY PETERSON, RVT
*Feral Cat Program Manager,*
The Humane Society of the United States
*President,* Cat Writers' Association

# PREFACE

Face the feline facts. Cats put the C in clever, the A in attitude, the T in tenacious, and the S in "so what." Don't expect them to apologize or to grovel — leave that to those gotta-please dogs. Cats pride themselves on being candid about what they want, when they want it.

Without a high-priced marketing team or a publicity-generating headline act in Las Vegas, cats have steadily and quietly overcome man's so-called best friend in terms of numbers and popularity worldwide. In the United States alone, cats outnumber dogs at 90.5 million to 74 million. People may say, "My dog really loves me," but they absolutely gush when they declare, "I'm crazy about my cat and I think she adores me too."

We live for their full-throttle purrs, their warmth in our laps, and their amusing antics. Still, felines can be funny, fussy, frustrating, and even a bit freaky. You may wonder why your cat digs her claws into your lap while she's cuddling. Perhaps you are stymied by your Persian's preference for using your pillow instead of her litter box. What's the deal on hairballs, bringing home dead birds, and nibbling on earlobes, anyway?

You may be puzzled and perplexed as you try to figure out why cats do what they do. That's why I wrote this book. Please regard *The Cat Behavior Answer Book* as your guide to unlocking the mysteries behind how cats think and act. I've collected the questions presented here during appearances on television and radio pet shows, at public speaking presentations, as the editor of *Catnip*, and as a former pet columnist for *Prevention*. Once people discover what I do for a living — and that two cats manage my home — they unleash their questions. *Why does my cat . . . ? How can I get my cat to stop . . . ? What is the best way to teach my cat to . . . ?* I hear from people at bookstores, at weddings, in supermarket lines, and even at dog parks.

A friend jokingly calls me Dr. Doo, short for Doctor Doolittle, because of the number of times she has witnessed me talking through solutions with a confused cat owner. Of course, I'm not a doctor. I don't even play one on TV. But I am a pet expert who regularly works with the very best in the fields of veterinary medicine and companion-animal behavior. I'm dedicated to providing you with the feline facts and practical solutions to your pussycat problems.

So, nix the notion that you can use "canine psychology" on your feline pal. What may work on your lovable Labrador won't work on your attention-demanding Abyssinian. Instead, please paw through these pages with an open mind and a willingness to be enlightened and educated. The legendary Doctor Doolittle talked to the animals. I'm here to deliver straight talk to you.

Paws Up!

*Arden Moore*

# ACKNOWLEDGMENTS

I wish to thank all the veterinarians, animal behaviorists, animal-shelter officials, talented individuals from the Cat Fanciers' Association and the Winn-Feline Foundation, plus the feline fans who generously shared their time, talents, and ideas in this book. Special gratitude to my team of feline behavior experts Joan Miller, Alice Moon-Fanelli, and Arnold Plotnick, as well as my editor, Lisa Hiley. Together, we can reach out and improve the lives of cats everywhere.

# PART I

# Feeling Fine about Being Feline

Ah, the life of a cat. It all seems so, well, purr-fect. Guaranteed meals. Plenty of time for napping. A personal assistant to tidy up your litter box. It is easy to feel a tinge of envy for our felines, but how much do we really know about them?

For starters, we may adore our furry friends, but the ancient Egyptians literally worshipped them. Centuries later, the tide had turned completely and the superstitious inhabitants of merry Old England burned thousands of them at the stake. Loved and loathed — that's been the cat's fate through the centuries. Today, more cats than dogs roost in American households.

In this section, I discuss many aspects of being a cat. For one thing, they like to ponder. After all, they waited an extra 10,000 years or so after dogs were domesticated before deigning to hang out with humans. They like to pounce, which explains how your ankle may be mistaken for a heavy-footed mouse in the hallway. They will lure you with purring to obtain a cozy lap, a fishy treat, or a nice scratch under the chin.

Cunning, candid, and clever — cats have these characteristics and more. Read on!

# Real Smarty Cat

**Q** Our household contains a Border collie, a poodle, and an Abyssinian. Those two dog breeds are known for their intelligence, but my Aby, aptly named Mensa, is no slouch when it comes to brainpower either. She comes on cue, walks on a leash, and goes to the kitchen and sits politely when asked if she wants a treat. How smart are cats and how do they learn?

**A** If there were a pet version of the popular game show *Jeopardy!,* your trio would trounce the competition, paws down. There is a lot of brainpower packed in that furry bunch, and you may not be surprised to hear that cats learn similarly to dogs and people.

Cats possess both short-term and long-term memories. That explains how they head for the litter box or food bowl kept in the same locale (long-term) or adjust if these feline necessities have been moved to a different room (short-term). Just like people and dogs, cats learn by observing, imitating, and trial and error.

Mensa may act like a dog when she performs those tricks on cue, but cats are big believers in the what's-in-it-for-me philosophy. Whereas dogs tend to perform to please us and to reap the treats, cats decide what they'll do and when they'll do it. If they can reasonably determine that you will come through with an acceptable reward, then they may participate in coming when called, sitting for a treat, or doing some other trick.

Cats also learn by paying close attention to what's going on in the house. For example, some smart cats watch their owners open doors and then try to duplicate that feat. A friend of mine has a Siamese who learned how to paw the doorknob that opens into the garage. To keep her cat from fleeing when the garage door opens (fortunately, Sheba has not discovered the location of the garage door opener mounted on the wall), my friend had to add a deadbolt lock to this door.

Evolution plays a role in how each species behaves. For instance, your two dogs may dig a shallow hole in your backyard on a hot, humid day as a way to cool their bellies. This instinctive behavior has been passed on from one canine generation to another. Cats, however, aren't hardwired to dig to cool down. Their paws aren't as suited for clawing up the earth. They are more apt to seek a shaded secluded place where they can keep an eye on predators while cooling their bodies. And, being the fastidious groomers they are, they are not so keen about rolling in the dirt and getting their coats messy.

Finally, cats are masters at manipulating us. Creatures of habit, they tap into their powers of observation and learning by association to use the household routine to their advantage. Callie, my calico, has trained me better than I care to admit. At least once a day, while I am working at the dining room table, she perches on a step midway down the staircase, poses charmingly while looking at me with soft eyes, and emits a soft mew. That's my cue to get up from the dining room chair, open the pantry door, and dole out a pinch or two of her favorite dried fish treat.

Of course, she didn't come down the stairs one day thinking, "I want a treat and I know how to get one," but the first time she paused and mewed at me on the stairs, and I jumped up to bring her a treat, she knew she was onto something good. Her position is strategic — it is at the same level as the pantry door. I know I'm being manipulated but happily comply. Callie is clever enough to recognize my weak spot and works it to her advantage. Who's the truly intelligent being now?

## Savoring Sleepy Times

**Q** Gracie, my gray-striped tabby, has quite a life. It seems that she sleeps all night and most of the day. I wish I could log half the amount of sleep she does. She does engage with me in brief play sessions, and she loves mealtime. She seems quite content, but I'm wondering if this much sleep is normal for a cat.

**A** Cats do love a good night's sleep and plenty of pleasant daytime naps. They are truly the Rip van Winkles of the world, averaging 17 to 18 hours of sleep each day, or about two-thirds of their entire lives. They sleep about twice as much as most other mammals, but they're not complaining.

How many hours they sleep each day is influenced by their age (fast-growing kittens tend to sleep more than adult cats), how safe they feel (sharing a home with a cat-pursuing dog would keep most cats awake and weary), and the weather (which explains why your cat carves a tunnel under your bedspread to snooze in during a snow storm).

You mention that Gracie seems content. Make sure that you are not confusing contentment with boredom. Bored cats sleep more than cats who interact and play with people and other pets in the home. So encourage those play sessions every day. Even five or ten minutes will activate her brain, work her muscles, and give her some cool memories to take with her when she dozes off into dreamland.

## TEST YOUR CAT'S IQ

Just how smart is your cat? One informal way to test your cat's intelligence is to evaluate his ability to discern *object permanence.* Originally designed to study cognitive development in children, this test can be applied to cats.

Show your cat an object in plain view, such as a toy mouse. Then hide the mouse by placing a file folder or other solid object in front of it. To be ranked with an 18-month-old child, your cat should know to look behind the object for the mouse, rather than thinking it has disappeared entirely once out of sight.

Super-smart cats, capable of thinking like a two-year-old child, will also be able to follow the trajectory of an object that moves out of view. In other words, these cats should be able to predict where a live mouse that scoots out of sight under a sofa will reappear and use that knowledge to pounce as the mouse reappears.

# Diving into Dreamland

**Q** I love watching my cat sleep. He moves a lot and even makes little squeaking sounds at times. His legs quiver and his whiskers move. Is he dreaming?

**A** Cats do dream, but we can only speculate on the subject matter. It might be that your cat is reliving the brilliant capture of a wayward fly buzzing near a sunny window or a particularly speedy sprint down the hallway. Perhaps he is recalling with amusement how he charmed that final piece of broiled tuna off your dinner plate and into his own bowl.

**FELINE FACT**

Cats are champion sleepers, but bats and opossums actually log more *zzzzs*. Those animals average 20 hours of sleep each day.

We do have scientific evidence that cats dream. As with humans, feline sleep falls into two types — REM (rapid eye movement, which is when dreams happen), and non-REM (deep sleep). You will know your cat is in REM sleep because he is apt to twitch his legs, wiggle his whiskers, and subtly move his eyes behind his closed eyelids.

Studies using electroencephalograms (EEGs) to read brain activity in sleeping cats have indicated that cats are in the REM sleep stage for about 30 percent of their sleeping time and that their brain wave patterns during REM are similar to ours. In comparison, we spend about 20 percent of our sleep time in the REM stage (although human babies spend up to 80 percent in REM).

When cats are not dreaming, they are in the deep sleep phase. This is the time when the body goes to work repairing and regenerating bones and muscles and bolstering the immune system to fend off disease. The only movement you can detect during this sleep stage is the quiet up and down of breathing.

## The Five Feline Senses

**Q** I know my cat, Cleo, hears much better than I do. She can be in a deep sleep on the second floor but will scoot down the stairs when she hears me opening the refrigerator door. That's where I keep her favorite treat — small pieces of broiled chicken. By the time I open up the lid of the container, she is affectionately rubbing against my leg. But sometimes Cleo doesn't seem to notice a toy mouse when it is right under her nose. When it comes to the five senses, how do cats compare with people?

**A** You're right that cats can hear much better than humans. If I whispered that fact in one room while you and Cleo were in another room, I would bet the mortgage that Cleo would pick up my words and you wouldn't. In fact, cats hear even better than dogs. They can hear sounds in the ultrasonic range, that is, at very high frequencies.

Sound is caused by vibrations, and the number of vibrations produced per second is called "frequency." Frequency is measured in hertz (Hz), with one hertz equal to one vibration per second. Cats can hear up to 100,000 Hz, compared to dogs at between 35,000 and 40,000 Hz and humans at up to 20,000 Hz.

Why can cats hear so much better than we can? First, take a look at the design of the feline ear. Those cone-shaped wonders can rotate like mini satellite dishes to hone in on sounds. With their ability to pick up higher frequencies, cats can detect the squeaks of a trespassing mouse in the house far faster than we do. Now, let's run down the four other senses and see how we stack up against our feline friends.

**THE NOSE KNOWS.** Cats learn about their environment by sniffing out facts. They pack about 200 million odor-sensitive cells in their nostrils, compared with our paltry 5 million. The feline nose does more than sniff out food morsels on the kitchen floor. Cats use their noses to communicate with other cats. Each time a cat rubs his scent glands from his head or paws on an object, he is leaving a feline business card for other cats to sniff and interpret.

**TOUCHY-FEELY.** Cats rely on their whiskers and paws to scout out their surroundings. You may be surprised to learn that whiskers are found not only on a cat's face but also on the backs of their front legs. They use whiskers as antennae, touching objects around them and determining if they can squeeze through tight openings. Special sensory whiskers called "vibrissae" help cats to stalk prey in dim light and to navigate. That said, there are some notable exceptions among feline breeds who maneuver quite nicely without long whiskers. For example, the Cornish Rex and the American Wirehair sport curly, short whiskers, while the Devon Rex has hardly any and the Sphynx lacks whiskers entirely. All of these breeds are fast and agile despite their short or missing whiskers.

**TASTE ISN'T EVERYTHING.** Cats have a reputation for being finicky eaters, and there is a scientific explanation. Cats have only about 473 taste buds compared to the more than 9,000 we possess. Because feline taste buds are few in number and poorly developed, cats depend more on their sense of smell than taste. They do not adopt the canine motto of "eat first, ask later" when it comes to food.

**THE EYES HAVE IT.** Finally, the reason Cleo may be missing that toy mouse right under her nose is because it is not moving. When it comes to the sight sense, cats surpass us in seeing movement due to their superior peripheral vision. Their pupils can dilate wider to capture more of a panoramic view than we can. However, they can be a bit myopic and not actually see what's literally under their noses, like that toy mouse, because they have a blind spot right under their chins.

So, if you're keeping score, it's Cats 4, Humans 0, with a possible tie for vision. I guess we should be grateful that we have something cats don't have — thumbs.

---

# Predator or Prey?

**Q** I love watching my three cats bat around toy mice and chase the feathers on a wand toy. Why is their hunting instinct so strong after they have been domesticated for thousands of years?

**A** While we usually think of cats as mighty hunters, they actually fill the role of both prey and predator, depending on the other species involved. Let's start with the predator part. All cats, from a mighty lion to that sweet kitty on your lap, are genetically programmed to hunt. In keeping with their size, cats focus on small mammals and birds. Interestingly, most biologists regard cats as small mammal experts and bird opportunists because cats tend not to be very good at catching birds unless the birds are sick, young, or ground nesting.

Predatory behavior is mostly innate, and kittens early on show a tendency to chase moving objects and to pounce on littermates. Just like us, they learn through trial and error, and their play sessions help them increase their speed and refine their leaping abilities.

Their moms also teach them by example. Outdoor cats often bring home a dead mouse or bird to their litter and eat it in front of the kittens to demonstrate needed behaviors. She will then present a dead animal to the kittens to eat themselves, and, finally, will bring home a nearly dead creature for the kittens to finish off. These experiences hone their hunting and killing skills. For indoor cats, the prey happens to be a store-bought toy or perhaps your pink slipper. But the lessons learned are the same, and many cats who never see a mouse or a bird until adulthood quickly figure out how to catch and kill their prey.

When the tables are turned and cats become the prey, they tap into their survival skills and the fight-or-flight mind-set. Outdoor cats are at risk not only from neighborhood dogs; even in suburban areas they often fall victim to coyotes, hawks, and other predators. Their first response is usually to flee if at all possible, either diving into a hiding place or scooting up a tree. A cornered cat can fight fiercely, however, as many a startled (and scratched) dog has discovered. The very tools that make them effective predators become their best defense. That must be where the phrase "to fight tooth and claw" comes from!

## CAT GEOMETRY AND PERSONALITIES

When searching for a kitten or cat to adopt, how can you tell if your selection will be a lap lounger, a shy cat, or an adventure seeker? Pedigreed (purebred) cats tend to have certain characteristic personality traits, though individuals within breeds may be very different. With the typical shelter cat, personality clues may be linked to the shape of the cat's face.

Kit Jenkins, program manager for PetSmart Charities, has spent more than 20 years studying the behavior of cats and dogs in animal shelters. She has developed a theory of cat face geometry, which is based on the fact that feline faces usually fall into one of three physical shapes: square, round, or triangle. While noting that genetics and life experiences play major roles in how cats think and act, Jenkins contends that personality is also influenced by a cat's physical shape. Here's how she describes the various types.

◆ **SQUARE.** These cats are big and solid with square faces and rectangular bodies. Think Maine Coon.

Jenkins dubs them the "retrievers of the cat world." Eager to please, square cats tend to be affectionate and love to snuggle and give head-butts.

◆ **ROUND.** These cats sport flat faces, large eyes, circular heads, and rounded bodies. Think Persian or Burmese. These types might be called the

"lap dogs" of the feline world. They tend to be low-energy, easily frightened, submissive cats who gently display their affection to trusted family members.

*(continued)*

◆ **TRIANGULAR.** These are
sleek, long, lanky cats
with big ears and faces
that narrow at the nose.
Think Siamese or Cornish
Rex. Jenkins calls them
"the herding dogs of the
cat world." Triangle cats are curious, smart, athletic,
and chatty, and they thrive in active households.

Jenkins has shared her personality theory with shelter workers, animal trainers, and behaviorists all over North America. Animal behaviorists and veterinarians say her observations serve as another tool in helping people find a cat who meets their lifestyle and personality. Although just a theory, Jenkins's observations have been supported by her peers; to date, though, nothing has been published in a scientific journal.

When I applied Jenkins's cat geometry theory to my own feline trio, I gained some insight into their individual ways. I own one of each personality shape — the only thing these three have in common is that all were strays who charmed their way into my heart and my house.

◆ Little Guy is my square-faced feline. At age 19, this brown-striped tabby is Mr. Mellow. He spends his afternoons sleeping on my office desk while I work. He always answers to my whistle and loves to give me a head-to-head greeting.

◆ Callie is my round-faced calico. This 12-year-old craves a quiet, consistent routine. She shyly shows affection by lightly brushing against my leg but darts away from sudden noises and avoids visitors with booming voices.

◆ Murphy is my triangle-faced cat. I can count on this high energy, sable-colored 8-year-old to greet all visitors and supervise all workmen in the house. She chases airborne paper wads, paws at the bubbles in my bath, and loves her daily stroll on her harness and leash.

Math wasn't my favorite subject in school, but thanks to this body-shape theory, I've finally found a way to put geometry to a practical use.

# Glow in the Dark Eyes

**Q** When I walk around my house at night in dimly lit rooms, sometimes I am a bit spooked when I see my cat. Precious is a sweet Siamese, but at night her eyes seem to glow red in the dark, giving off a devilish look. I seem to notice this most after I've watched a scary movie on TV. What causes her eyes to glow like this?

**A** Timing is everything. You are more apt to be a little jumpy after watching a horror movie, but don't worry about Precious. She is not possessed by the devil. Her large, round pupils are designed to operate far better in low light conditions and in the dark than our eyes are. As hunters who are active at dawn and dusk — the best times to stalk prey — cats can actually see as well in pitch black as we can see in full moonlight.

Holding your cat in your lap, take a look at her eyes some evening under a bright lamp. Notice that the pupils are elliptical in shape, compared to our circular ones. In the lamplight, the pupils become narrow slits to protect the sensitive retinas from damage. Now turn the lamp off and notice that her pupils dilate to accommodate the lower lighting. In very dim light, the pupils will fill her eyes, making them look almost completely black.

As for that red glow, it is caused by light reflected from a layer of tissue called the "tapetum lucidum," which lines the back of the eyeball behind the retina. It acts like a mirror, reflecting light that was not absorbed the first time it passed through the retina back through the eyes onto the light sensor cells in the retina. The result is an eerie glow as your cat's eyes catch a beam of light in a dark room.

**FELINE FACT**

Tapetum lucidum, the reflective layer in cats' eyes, is a Latin phrase that means "bright carpet."

Interestingly, some feline eyes glow green rather than red depending on the color of the cat's eyes. Blue eyes, which your Siamese has, glow red, while golden and green eyes cast a green glow at night.

## Facts on Feline Love

**Q** My super-sweet kitty, Bubba, likes to cuddle with me and follow me around the house. He is very friendly and affectionate, and of course I love him to pieces. This may be a silly question, but I've always wondered if cats are capable of loving us or are they just being nice because we give them food and shelter?

**A** That's not a silly question, but it doesn't have an easy answer. I would be able to give you a more definitive response if I could speak cat and ask the feline world directly. Cats are candid creatures and I'm certain they would reply honestly.

Without that ability, however, defining feline love can be tricky. What we do know is that cats clearly express emotions. They get angry and they show fear. They display contentment and express excitement. As for interpreting cat love, cats definitely form attachments with people in their lives who make them feel safe and who shower them with attention.

Cats convey affection toward their people in a number of ways, including delivering soft-eyed winks by half-closing both eyes at once, twitching an upright tail, and delivering head bonks also known as bunting. The next time you lock eyes with your cat, try giving him a few soft winks. I bet he returns the favor. And notice that when he sees you enter a room or hears your voice, his tail probably pops straight up in the air with the tip twitching just a bit. See if he expresses affection by purposely bumping the top of his head against your forehead, hands, or shins.

When I first adopted Little Guy, he was a young tiger-striped stray who camped out on my front porch each morning and evening in hope of scoring a free meal. I put food in a bowl for him though I wasn't sure if I wanted another cat. But every time I bent down to pet him, he beat me to the punch by quickly stretching his body and bumping his head against my hand, accompanied by full-throttle purring.

Little Guy knew what he was doing. He was showing he liked me and as a result, he won me over. Sometimes, the timing of feline affection is not ideal, such as when your cat jumps on your bed and head-slams your forehead when you're sound asleep.

But as you know, true love doesn't care about time. Take it as a compliment that Bubba follows you around and likes to cuddle.

## DO CATS HAVE A FUNNY BONE?

One of my favorite humorists and fan of cats is Dena Harris, the "Erma Bombeck of cat writers." The author of *Lessons in Stalking: Adjusting to Life with Cats,* Harris created a Top 10 list (adapted below) to show that our feline friends do indeed see the humorous aspects of sharing their lives with us:

1. Our astonishing lack of hair

2. The way we harbor the illusion that we stand even the smallest chance of winning a staring contest against them (Hint: Cats blink only because they feel sorry for us.)

3. Our ability to pass through a sunbeam without dropping unconscious to the floor

4. That we appear *not* to consider a live mouse the finest form of in-home entertainment

5. The way we fold clothes warm from the dryer instead of diving headfirst into them

6. The time we spend working to remove the glorious trail of cat hair from around the house when they know they can replace it all in 6.4 seconds

7. That we think those decapitated rodents left on the back porch are presents for *us*

8. That we ignore the primary uses of the computer and TV, both of which are for napping

9. That we choose *not* to walk around on top of the countertops, which is where all the best views are to be had, not to mention treats

10. Our never-ending devotion and eternal servitude to them (Actually, cats don't so much laugh at this last one as encourage it.)

# Guilt-ridden or Just Plain Bored?

**Q** Increased work demands have recently called for me to travel a lot more, and my cat, Keeper, a beautiful Bengal, is sometimes home alone for a night. I have friends who stop by to feed him if I am gone more than overnight, but he is still alone more than he used to be. When I came home from my last trip, he had shredded the toilet paper, clawed a corner of my couch, and tipped over a container on my desk that sent paper clips flying all over the floor. When I saw this, I marched up to him and yelled at him. He fled and hid under the bed for a while. Are cats capable of plotting revenge, and do they feel guilt when they do something we don't want them to do?

**A** In the animal kingdom, humans have a monopoly on feeling guilty. Cats, dogs, and the rest of our animal companions do not experience or express guilt. It is tempting to anthropomorphize your cat, giving him human reasons for his misdeeds and for running away when you chastised him. But the truth is that guilt is self-reflective, an emotion only people feel, according to top psychologists.

Guilt is a human response to behavior that we recognize as wrong or socially unacceptable. Cats do not have the capacity for that type of abstract thinking. However, cats are definitely capable of experiencing fear and submission. It is easy to confuse feline fear with guilt.

In Keeper's case, he is most likely bored by those long stretches of being home alone. Bored cats, especially active breeds like Bengals, will look for ways to amuse themselves, even if that something (clawing couches, turning toilet paper into confetti, and pawing piles of paper clips) is not desirable from your point of view. In other cats, these actions could illustrate separation anxiety. Whether a cat is bored or anxious depends on his temperament and relationship with his owner.

Keeper cowered and hid under the bed when you yelled because he was frightened of your angry voice, not because he was feeling guilty about his "bad" behavior. He had no idea why you were angry, only that you were acting scary and threatening.

My recommendation is first to take away feline temptations. When you're not home, shut the bathroom door, put a covering on your couch to stop his claws, and tidy your desk. Next, provide Keeper with acceptable outlets for his boredom. These might include battery-operated toys that move when he touches them, a sturdy window perch for him to keep tabs on the neighborhood, or a circular trackball toy that encourages him to paw at the ball. You could try turning on the radio or television to add some sound to ease his solitude. There are videos of fish and birds and other cat-enticing images that might occupy his attention in your absence.

When you do come home from those business trips, ignore any messes and greet Keeper with happiness and affection. Spend some time playing with him and petting him so that he doesn't feel alone even with you back in the house. You may discover that he comes rushing up to greet you after an absence.

---

# Why Cats Mask Their Pain

**Q** I was shocked the other day to discover a deep gash near my longhaired cat's hind leg. When my veterinarian shaved the area and examined it, she told me it was an infected cat bite. She cleaned the wound, closed it with stitches, and prescribed medication. It was obvious that Freckles was in a lot of pain, but she never gave me any clues that she was hurting. Why wouldn't my cat let me know that she was hurt?

**A** Cats are masters at masking their pain, because their survival might depend on it. As small creatures who are vulnerable to larger predators, cats can't afford to disclose any weakness. With obvious injuries or illness, they become easy targets, which explains why they instinctively mask signs of pain or sickness, even from the people who love and protect them. Unfortunately, this is why many of my veterinarian friends relate stories of clients who bring in cats who are just "not acting right" only to discover that their pets are in full-blown stages of cancers or kidney failure or other serious health problems.

Since cats prefer to hide any signs of weakness, we need to be attuned to any subtle signs of illness. Here are some clues to look for and to report to your veterinarian.

- Inappropriate elimination
- Changes in eating habits
- Eating litter
- Sudden weight loss
- Bad breath
- Changes in normal activity level
- Changes in sleep habits
- Changes in social interactions
- Changes in grooming habits
- Becoming more vocal
- Suddenly hiding and declining attention

## CAT BITE CARE

An undetected bite wound can cause an abscess, which is a buildup of fluid and debris under the skin. Wounds like these nearly always require medical attention, because cats have bacteria in their mouths that can cause infection.

If you discover a bite wound and cannot get to the veterinary clinic right away, wrap your cat in a towel to make it easier and safer to clean the wound. Use hydrogen peroxide or warm water to flush the puncture area. Try to clip away as much hair from around the wound as possible and leave the area open to breathe. Do not clip if you feel unsure or if your cat resists. If the wound is bleeding profusely, apply a compress.

Then bring your cat to your veterinarian as soon as possible. You don't want to risk further damage or a serious infection.

If you are bitten by a cat, be very alert for signs of infection. It is hard to clean a puncture wound properly, and you may well need antibiotics if the bite is deep enough.

# Cat Scratch Fever

**Q** I've always had fish and turtles and finally decided that I was ready for a more complicated, interactive pet. I recently adopted a big orange tabby from the local animal shelter. Gus is great, but he loves to claw and tear at his scratching post. Luckily for me, he leaves my couch alone. Why does he have this need to scratch?

**A** Bravo! With no disrespect intended for the fish and turtles in your life, I am happy that you are ready and willing to enjoy the perks of feline companionship. And I am happy to hear that you adopted from a local shelter because you have given a homeless cat another chance.

Scratching, as you have discovered, is one of the signature actions of cats. Even declawed cats will perform scratching gestures. You're lucky that Gus adores his scratching post and not your expensive sofa. Cats scratch for a couple of reasons. One reason is to keep their claws in shape — what I call a "peti-cure." Those scratching sessions remove the dead outer nail covering and hone the claw's shape and sharpness, keeping Gus prepared to defend himself or to pounce on a passing mouse.

However, the paramount reason cats scratch has to do with turf talk. When Gus scratches, he is leaving a feline business card, if you will. He not only leaves physical marks, but also the scratching action releases a scent from the sebaceous glands in his paws that communicates to other cats — and to himself — that this is his domain.

You mention that you are grateful he only scratches the cat post, but I'll bet if you pay close attention, you will discover that old Gus is pawing and rubbing his face to leave his scents on doorways and wall corners. It appears as a dirty, oily discoloration on the walls and doors. (See Cat-to-Cat Communication, page 76, for more on scent marking.)

---

# The Need to Knead

**Q** Whenever I'm sitting down, my cat will climb into my lap, circle around, plop down, and busily start to push her paws (and claws) up and down on my legs. I call it her happy dance. She sometimes does the same thing on my bed before settling down for the night. Why does she do this?

**A** The feline ritual of rhythmically pumping their paws up and down begins at birth. Newborns push their paws around their mother's nipples while they suckle to hasten the flow of milk. Even after they are weaned, kittens remember the happy feeling of a full belly that came with kneading and nursing. As adults, "making biscuits," as I like to call it, brings them a sense of comfort. It is a way for cats to convey joy and delight in having you in their lives. If you regularly clip your cat's nails, you might avoid the pain of her nails plunging into your leg.

Some cats can go a little overboard, though. Some drool while kneading, and others become so enthusiastic that they drive their sharp claws into human legs. If your cat is turning you into a pincushion and regular nail clipping sessions aren't making it less painful for you, you can stop this behavior from becoming an unpleasant habit by simply standing up and walking away. After being ousted from your cozy lap a few times, your cat is apt to tone down her need to knead.

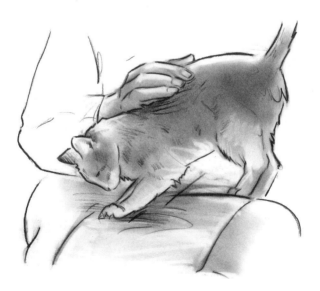

# Taming Tara's Terrors

ACCEPTING AN INVITATION to address veterinary school students enrolled in a shelter medicine class, I knew the power of showing, not simply telling. So I visited a local animal shelter in search of a perfect "demo" cat. I found her — a black, longhaired cat named Tara who hissed and crouched in the back corner of her cage.

Although Tara had entered the shelter as a trapped stray just the day before and lashed out at any attempts to touch her, she displayed signs that she may not have lived on the streets all her life. Her coat was fairly shiny, indicating that she had been grooming herself. She displayed a good weight, showed no signs of battle scars and — the biggest giveaway — was not pregnant or lactating as is the case with most feral females.

Any cat entering a shelter may feel temporarily threatened by the strange sounds, smells, and typical shelter handling with gloves or cat-grabbing equipment. A truly feral cat is not social or touchable and is not considered adoptable. A frantic cat is one who has known humans but is in a state of fear-induced panic.

Using Tara as an example, I shared techniques with the veterinary students on ways to help scared cats such as Tara gain self-confidence through repeated pleasurable handling and socialization from shelter staff and volunteers. As cats feel less stressed in the shelter, they begin to show their true personalities, thereby increasing their chances for adoption.

On my first visit, I avoided making direct eye contact with Tara's angry eyes because cats view prolonged staring as a sign of imminent attack. After several sessions spent just talking to her, I lightly touched her with a soft feather teaser, brushing it over her back, neck, head, nose, and eyes. She responded without making a hiss. The next time, she stood up and arched her neck toward the feather, a sign she was developing trust in me.

Knowing it was time to touch her, I slowly took her out of the cage, hindquarters first, and placed her four feet on a small table, so she would not feel clutched. I purposely faced her away from me, so she could observe the entire room without feeling trapped. Speaking softly, I was able to lightly touch her coat.

At my presentation, this once-scared black cat amazed the students by behaving in a social and friendly manner. Tara now lives in a happy home with people who adore her. Her owners find it hard to believe that Tara was once a hissing, swatting cat in a shelter, because she is now so sweet and loving.

*Contributed by Joan Miller, all-breed judge*

# Four-Legged Gymnasts

**Q** I am embarrassed to admit that I would sometimes hold my childhood cat belly up over my
head and let him fall. I was amazed at how he could
twist his body and land on his four feet with ease. I have
much more respect for cats as an adult, but I am still
intrigued by their athleticism. How do cats manage to
maneuver their bodies and land safely?

**A** My advice is never to challenge a cat to a game of
Twister. He will win every time, paws down. A flexible musculoskeletal system and a strong sense of balance
enable airborne cats to right themselves rapidly and grace-
fully and, most times, safely. You may be surprised to learn
that cats don't have collarbones, but they do have flexible
backbones with five more vertebrae than humans, allowing them to twist and turn in midair.

Their superior sense of balance and coordination comes
from the vestibular apparatus, the fluid-filled canal in the
ear that allows both humans and cats to remain upright
when walking and to figure out where the ground is in
relation to the body. When a cat falls, the fluid activates
tiny hairs in the ear canal, allowing the cat to determine its
body position and identify which way is up.

Studies on falling cats have discovered that felines who
fall from heights of seven stories or fewer face greater
injury than those falling from greater heights. In fact,

cats have survived falls from as high as eighteen stories. The explanation is that after falling five stories or so, a cat reaches terminal velocity. On a longer fall, it has time to right itself, relax its muscles, and spread out its limbs like a flying squirrel to slow down its rate of speed.

The actual movements from the start of the fall to the four-on-the-floor finish are quite ballet-like. First, the falling cat rotates its head and the front of its body to bring its legs underneath its body. The hind end then moves into alignment. Just as he lands, he brings the front legs closer to his face to absorb some of the impact and bends his back legs to prepare for the jolt.

As agile as cats are, they do not always land on their feet. Cats have suffered injury from falls off of countertops and two-story balconies. That's why I strongly urge all cat owners to make sure that all window screens are sturdy and will not pop open from the weight of a cat perched on the sill. And don't let your cat roam unsupervised on a balcony. All it takes is for one sparrow to fly by and your bird-chasing cat could leap up and over the balcony ledge in determined pursuit.

# Successful Therapy Cats

**Q** Now that I'm retired from teaching, I enjoy taking my certified therapy dog to nursing homes and children's hospitals. But some people I visit like cats better than they like dogs. My cat, Kai, is a young, friendly Maine Coon. Visitors to my home always remark how comfortable they feel around Kai. He likes to ride in the car and happily travels with me when I visit family and friends. Can cats make good therapy animals?

**A** Being greeted by a friendly therapy animal can do wonders to boost the outlook and even the physical health of those in nursing homes and hospitals. Dogs do make up the majority of certified therapy animals, but cats are increasing in numbers. Felines are small and easy to pick up, and possess one major advantage over dogs: the soothing sound of purring.

Kai's easygoing style and desire to greet people are two key traits needed for therapy cats. That he enjoys traveling is an added plus, since most cats prefer to be homebodies and don't like adjusting to new surroundings. Generally speaking, Maine Coons are gentle, affectionate giants who would probably take to therapy work. Some Persians also make good therapy cats because they tend to be calm and patient, and they definitely enjoy being showered with affection. Tonkinese, a less common breed, are noted as being ideal therapy cats because they are outgoing with strangers and like to sit on laps. But there are always exceptions within breeds, and of course there are many random bred cats who succeed as therapy cats.

Contact a therapy animal organization in your area that provides certified programs. (See resources, page 314, for suggestions.) Although each program differs, the ground rules call for cats to be at least one year old; fully updated on all their vaccinations; in good health; and able to tolerate travel, loud noises, crowds, strange smells, and frequent handling. They must be good-natured about being poked at or pulled on, and comfortable with people of all ages.

To ensure Kai's safety, I recommend you train him to wear a harness and walk on a leash, rather than relying on a carrier. He will definitely win admiration if he can strut into a hospital room on a leash. Cats able to perform tricks such as paw waving, sitting up on their hind legs, and jumping into open arms on cue will make a great impression as well. Of course, possessing a strong, steady purr only enhances his popularity among people in need of a little TLC (tender loving cat).

## Why Whiskers?

**Q** My young daughter recently took her kindergarten scissors and trimmed all the whiskers off our cat. Of course I was very upset with her, because I know cats need their whiskers to find their way around, but I realize that I don't really know how they work. What happens when a cat loses his whiskers?

**A** Most people realize that whiskers serve as measuring tools for most breeds of cats. The width of the whiskers along the sides of the face sizes up small openings to alert them if their bodies can fit through without getting stuck. Perhaps that explains why my chubbiest cat, Murphy, sports the longest whiskers among my three cats. But as mentioned in Five Feline Senses, page 9, not all breeds rely on whiskers to help them navigate.

Whiskers serve other vital purposes. A cat uses the long, protruding whiskers along his muzzle to rotate and scan for signs of possible prey. What is amazing is that the whiskers don't have to actually touch an object for a cat to realize it is there. Bundles of nerves in the whiskers supply oodles of information to the cat's brain, delivering almost supersensory abilities. I often equate this feline "Spidey sense" to that of superhero Spiderman.

Cats also have delicate whiskers above their eyes. Like our eyelashes, these whiskers activate a blinking reflex that automatically shields their eyes from flying debris. Wispy whiskers under the chin

sense objects from below. Whiskers on the front legs assist in safe landings and to sense the presence of prey.

Whiskers also signal feline moods. Pay attention to your cat's whiskers when he goes on the alert or appears content. When relaxed, a cat's whiskers are held slightly to the side. But when a cat is intrigued or feels threatened, the whiskers automatically tense up and point forward.

Without his whiskers, your cat's sense of balance, depth perception, and warning systems can be altered slightly. Veterinarians recommend keeping a whiskerless cat inside until the whiskers grow back, which can take two or three months.

## WHISKERY FACTS

Whiskers are technically known as "vibrissae." Grab a magnifying glass and take a close-up look. A cat's whiskers are about twice as thick as the hair on their coat, and the roots of the whiskers are about three times deeper than hair roots. Cats sport from 8 to 12 long whiskers on each side of their upper lip. They lose a few whiskers at a time as part of the normal shedding process, never losing them all at once.

# Insights into Cat Shows

**Q** A friend of mine has three Havana Brown cats that she enters in cat shows. She has invited me to attend a show. I often watch dog shows on television, but I'm not at all sure how a cat show works. Can you give me some insight on what to expect and how to behave at a cat show?

**A** Dogs aren't the only animals who like to mug for a camera or strike a pose for a judge, and dog owners aren't the only people who like to show off their sleek, well-groomed, and highly pedigreed pets. You can learn a lot about cats by taking the time to attend a cat show.

The Cat Fanciers' Association Championship International show I attended drew more than 800 felines representing 41 breeds. It was a marvelous opportunity to see so many different cat breeds under one roof. True, cats do not vary as much in size or looks as their canine counterparts, but there is a great distinction between a Sphynx and a Maine Coon or between an Ocicat and a Ragdoll. I was surprised to discover that many show cats like to strut their stuff just as much as dogs do. Some even revel in a new feline event — indoor agility. (See Make Way for Feline Athletes, page 284.)

Most cat shows feature judging rings for seven different classes. Like dogs, cats are judged not against each other but against a written breed standard of perfection. Rather than trotting around the ring all at once, cats are brought to a particular area to be handled and inspected individually by the judge for each class. The seven main classes are listed below.

**KITTEN.** Unaltered or altered kittens too young for Championship classes

**CHAMPIONSHIP.** Unaltered, registered cats over eight months of age

**PREMIERSHIP.** Neutered or spayed, registered cats over eight months of age

**VETERAN.** Registered cats seven years or older

**PROVISIONAL.** Registered breeds with provisional standards established by CFA but not yet accepted for Championship competition

**MISCELLANEOUS.** Registered breeds not accepted for Provisional Breed competition

**HOUSEHOLD PET.** Any domestic kitten or altered cat not otherwise eligible

There are many ways to snag a ribbon at a cat show. Categories include best of color, best champion within a breed, and best of breed. There is even a separate competition called Junior Showmanship. This is a program to evaluate young participants' knowledge of cat care, breed history, and standards in an effort to encourage family involvement in cat show competitions.

As for being a spectator, there is a certain etiquette required of attendees. Some of the inside tips I can share are on the following page.

◆ Never touch a cat without the owner's permission. Not all cats like being handled by large numbers of strangers. Also, you don't want to risk passing germs from one cat to another or detracting from the cat's well-groomed appearance that took hours to achieve. Exhibitors will usually ask visitors to spray disinfectant/odor neutralizer on their hands before petting their cat.

◆ Time your photo-taking opportunities. Ask permission before snapping away at a captivating cat being groomed or in the judging ring.

◆ Don't engage in extended small talk with the cat show exhibitors. They are busy listening for their cats' numbers to be called to a judging ring and keeping their cats calm and well coiffed. Ask if they have time to answer a question or two, but let them initiate any lengthy conversation about their cats and their particular breed characteristics. Most do enjoy talking about cats when the time is right. Look for exhibitors wearing "Ask Me" buttons as these people are in the CFA Ambassador Program and they are always willing to answer questions or just "talk cats."

◆ Leave your feline friend at home. These shows are limited to cats competing for honors. And of course, no dogs are allowed!

What I like best about cat shows is that they are not limited to pedigreed cats. Most shows sponsor a Household Pet competition that is open to random bred cats at least four months old. The winners are judged for their overall coat and body condition, reflecting good health and cleanliness, as well as for their unique appearance and appealing personality. The agility competition is also open to all cats, pedigreed or random bred.

If you are interested in exhibiting your cat, you might be surprised to know that many cats, once exposed to the busy cat show environment, enjoy the process. Household Pet cats must be entered before the show; the club sponsoring the show will have information necessary to prepare your future star and make this a good experience.

I am also impressed that many cat show organizers work with local shelters and rescue groups to promote adoptions for cats in need of homes.

## THE FABULOUS FELINE FIVE

What do America's 90.5 million cats look like? A great many are "just cats" — tabbies, tigers, tortoiseshells, and tuxedos, both short- and longhaired. Of the 41 pedigreed breeds recognized by the Cat Fanciers' Association, keepers of the world's largest cat registry, these are the most popular breeds.

1. The Persian has held on to the top spot since 1871. People love his easygoing nature and admire the long silky fur that requires daily combing to keep it mat-free.

2. The all-American Maine Coon Cat overshadows most other breeds in terms of size and bulk, but has a gentle giant temperament. This breed is often referred to as dog-like in character. The long coat comes in a variety of gorgeous colors.

3. The Exotic resembles a Persian except for his coat, which is dense, soft, plush, and medium length, and does not require daily fussing over. He is sometimes called the "Persian in pajamas." People love his cherubic face, solid body, and calm, even temperament.

4. Known globally as the breed that loves to talk, the Siamese has long been one of the most easily identified breeds. People are drawn to the graceful, muscular build, the smooth, short coat, and matching "points" of dark color on the face, ears, legs and tail. The breed's loud, raspy yowls are definitely distinctive.

*(continued)*

5. The active, intelligent Abyssinian loves to be around people. The Aby makes a perfect match for people looking for plenty of inter-action with their feline pals. He is a regal beauty with a slightly rounded, wedge-shaped face, lithe body, and short, dense silky coat, which is ticked like a wild rabbit and comes in several colorful shades.

Rounding out the top 10 in order are the Ragdoll, Birman, American Shorthair, Oriental, and Sphynx. Now, I love the look and predictable personality traits of the pedigreed cats, but keep an open mind when you think about adopting a kitten or a cat. Consider the spontaneous beau-ties of the feline world without a pedigree that are known by the abbreviations DSH (domestic shorthair) and DLH (domestic longhair).

# Why So Few Cat Breeds?

**Q** I'm curious about why there are more than 150 recognized dog breeds but only 41 distinct cat breeds. Dogs can weigh 5 to 180 pounds, with a huge variety of ear, nose, and tail shapes, and many different types of coats. Cats pretty much weigh between 6 and 20 pounds, have essentially similar faces, and not as much variation as to fur. Why is there so much variety in dogs and so much similarity in cats?

**A** Good question. Dogs were domesticated thousands of years before cats even associated with humans because we needed canines to help us hunt, pull heavy sleds, herd our flocks, and other tasks. There has been incentive for people over hundreds of years to tweak the breeding of various dogs to better suit their needs. That explains why there is such a variety in size, temperament, and abilities among dogs.

Cats have primarily been kept as hunters and companions. Because they were not tapped to perform a laundry list of activities, there are not as many distinct breeds nor such a great range in weight or size among the feline population.

# Choosing a Kitten or a Cat

**Q** I want to adopt a cat from my local shelter, but as a first-time pet owner, I need some advice. Should I adopt a kitten or a grown cat? What should I look for in deciding among so many? How can I make sure the cat is a good match for me?

**A** These are important questions and you are wise to be thinking about them before you bring a cat home. As you prepare to welcome a new feline into your life, my main advice is to think long term. Think of it this way — you are likely to have this cat in your life much longer than you will have the car you drive. Sadly, people typically spend many hours picking out a vehicle they keep for four or five years but spend only a few minutes selecting a feline companion who may be part of their lives for 15 years or more.

You need to be honest about your lifestyle and personality, and also a bit selfish. Your new cat or kitten needs to match your lifestyle and your preferences. If you really want a shorthaired cat so you don't have to fuss over daily grooming, then please do not let a well-meaning friend talk you into adopting a longhaired cat, no matter how beautiful it is. If you like a cat to "talk back" at you, then seek out an active, chatty one, not a shy feline mime. Do you admire an independent spirit or would you prefer a cuddly lap cat? An adorable kitten is hard to resist, but do you have the time and patience for the high-energy antics that come with a youngster?

I recommend that you write out a checklist of what your "dream" cat looks like and acts like. Your mission: to seek a feline that best matches your list. There are hundreds of cats in your area needing a home, so don't be in a hurry. Take your time and you will be rewarded with a lifelong cat pal. Visit different shelters and look in local papers for groups that rescue cats. There are also breed rescue groups to contact if a pedigreed cat would be a good match for the desired temperament traits on your list.

Once you have assessed your needs, my advice is for you to be calm and passive in the shelter and see which cat chooses you as a good match. I trust cat intuition. That's how my cat Murphy picked me. She ran and hid whenever others tried to catch her, but would bounce out of the bushes and rub against my leg when I appeared.

When my friend Jim wanted to adopt a kitten years ago, I went with him to the local animal shelter. Jim is a big, brawny guy with a quiet nature. Each time he picked up a kitten, he felt awkward. He finally confessed that he didn't feel comfortable raising a tiny, bouncy kitten. In the end, he took home a pair of one-year-old littermates who lived with him for 17 years. These cats provided companionship for one another when Jim worked long hours. They played together and snuggled together for afternoon naps. Like Jim, if you are honest about your wants and needs, I'm sure you will find the perfect companion.

## CAT-PROOFING YOUR HOUSE

Adopting a new cat or kitten is fun and exciting. But make sure you temper that enthusiasm with a dose of safety. Here are 10 ways to ensure your cat enjoys home, safe home.

1. Keep antifreeze and other garage hazards away from your curious feline. Ingesting even one teaspoonful can be fatal to most cats.

2. Install baby locks on cabinets where you keep household cleaners and other sprays. Be cautious when taking any medicines and avoid dropping a pill where your pet might scarf it up, thinking it's a nice treat.

3. Keep needles, thread, and string off the ground. Some cats are also attracted to jewelry and shiny candy wrappers. Swallowing any of these can cause internal injuries.

4. Inspect your window screens to make sure they are sturdy.

5. Enclose electrical cords in PVC channels to keep chew-happy cats from harm.

6. Put plants out of reach. Nibbled leaves can cause stomach upset or even intestinal blockage, and some are poisonous to cats.

7. Check your dryer between laundry loads. Some cats like to nap in dark, warm places.

8. Bang on the hood of your car before driving away to startle away any cat that might have crawled onto the engine block to snooze.

9. Look around before you sit in a recliner or a rocking chair. A cat may be napping under the legs or inside the recliner.

10. Block off areas behind major appliances and heavy furniture, such as your refrigerator, couch, or a big bookcase — any place where your cat could become stuck.

# **Stray or Feral?**

**Q** A couple of skinny young cats have been hanging out in the alleyway behind our restaurant. They are foraging for scraps of food. At first, they dashed away when I came out the door. But since I've started to put out food and water for them, one of them is starting to trust me and to creep closer. The other one still flees at the sight of me. I'd like to adopt the friendlier cat, but how can I tell if a homeless cat is stray or feral?

**A** All around the world, caring people are putting out bowls of food and water on porches, alleys, and other places to provide nourishment to homeless cats. It can be challenging to distinguish between feral cats (those born in the wild who have had little or no interaction with humans) and stray cats (those who have lived with people but have become lost or been discarded).

But in your situation, you can help both cats. The one who seems more trusting of you is likely to be a stray cat who finds himself in the great outdoors and wishes he was safe inside a home. The second one appears to be feral — he has no desire to be stuck in a house with a human but is

## DONOR CAT ADOPTIONS

Consider adopting a cat who has served as a blood donor at a veterinary hospital. These cats typically are healthy, even tempered, and social. Plus, they have spent their first few years being true lifesavers to ill and injured cats. Donor cats, who are usually found as strays or given up by their owners, range from one to ten years in age. They weigh 10 pounds or more and live strictly indoors. All are rigorously screened for good health and all cats also receive echocardiograms to ensure their hearts are healthy.

If you live near a veterinary hospital, I urge you to give these very special cats your very special consideration.

strongly motivated to seek food, even if it is offered by a human being.

For the second one, I encourage you to contact a local cat rescue group and ask them if they can set out a humane trap (scented with tuna or other aromatic food as a lure). Some groups are also willing to let individuals borrow one of their traps.

Once the cat is in the trap, you can give him or her a wonderful gift by taking him to a veterinarian for a health exam and spay or neuter surgery. The treated cat is then returned to his outdoor home where other members of his colony live.

As for the stray cat who has captured your curiosity, and apparently your heart, avoid making any fast motions or speaking loudly around him. Your goal is to win him over

## ALLEY CAT ALLIES

Feral cats live in colonies where they interact with one another, but have no interest in living indoors with humans. They can survive by hunting and scavenging if they have adequate shelter and not too much competition for food, but are subject to illness, injury, and predation. And in just a year or two, the offspring of a couple of feral cats can overrun the neighborhood.

Concerned individuals are paying more attention to the status of feral cats, and efforts are growing to spay and neuter colonies to humanely address the overpopulation issue. Leading this effort is Alley Cat Allies, a Maryland-based, non-profit organization by displaying cat-accepting etiquette. Chances are that he will eventually approach you and allow you to gently touch him. It may take a few days or weeks, but go slowly with your introductions. If you are worried about his safety or his health, you might speed up the process by capturing him in a humane trap and taking him to a veterinarian for a complete head-to-tail examination before adopting him. Good luck!

that striving to educate people as well as cater to homeless cats. One way to keep feral cats healthy and to prevent them from spreading diseases or overpopulating is through Trap, Neuter, and Return (TNR) programs.

These cats are trapped humanely, given medical exams and necessary vaccinations, and spayed or neutered before being returned to their original locale. To keep tabs on which feral cat has already gone through the TNR procedure, the ear is notched or the tip of an ear is removed as an identifiable sign. For TNR colony management to be successful, volunteers must provide regular food, monitor the health of the colony, and watch for any newcomers.

# The Clever Korat

IMAGINE THE PLEASURE OF LIVING WITH a moving "museum piece" with a shimmering silver-tipped coat and large, luminous green eyes. The government of Thailand officially recognizes the Korat cat as a national treasure. An ancient manuscript, *Cat-Book Poems,* created during the Ayudha period of Thai history (AD 1350 to 1767) depicts "good luck" cats. Among them is the Si-Sawat, as Korats are called in Thailand. Their "hairs are smooth with roots like clouds and tips like silver" and their "eyes shine like dewdrops on a lotus leaf."

Among the purest of all breeds, the Korat's physical appearance has remained unchanged for centuries. Every Korat today is silver blue and all trace their ancestry to Thailand. It is conceivable that their unique breed-related personality traits could be a reflection of their rich heritage.

These cats have enjoyed centuries of close association with humans, particularly high-ranking Thai government officials, nobility, and representatives of foreign governments. Si-Sawats were cherished by their owners, regarded as good luck cats, and given as wedding gifts. Some people trained them to check for scorpions before the baby was placed in his crib.

Today's Korats are exceptionally bonded to their own family and home. They follow their owners around the house, communicating through a variety of expressive sounds. A Korat is a "listening" cat, always watching, deliberately cautious. The world revolves around a Korat, who generally prefers a quiet household and always expects people to do the adapting.

In describing Korats, the first attribute mentioned is usually intelligence. Most cats have smartness based on instinct, but Korats display ingenuity. They easily learn specific words, play fetch, and can get into any cabinet. Korat fanciers around the world enjoy exchanging examples of their cats' exceptional memories, ability to think, and problem-solving skills.

A couple in Seattle always took their Korat on boat trips. She was not allowed on the open deck unless she had on her harness and leash. When she wanted to join them on the deck, she would pick up her harness and carry it in her mouth to the porthole.

Korat kittens like to select their own owners. When a litter is shown to a potential owner, all of the kittens will be curious, but often one kitten decides this is "his" person and proceeds to climb in the lap, perhaps chew on the hair, and become irresistible, while the other littermates act aloof or shy.

These remarkable cats are still treasured as much for their winning personalities as for their stunning beauty.

*Contributed by Joan Miller, all-breed judge*

# Cats and Birds and Mice, Oh My!

**Q** In a *Brady Bunch*–style union, my new husband and I are trying to merge our teenagers as well as cats, birds, and mice under one roof. We are optimistically hoping for harmony. I have two curious cats. He has one talkative bird and a handful of pet mice. He has never owned a cat. I have never owned birds or mice. Can these different animals live in harmony with one another?

**A** Prevention is the key here. It is unlikely that your grown cats will come to regard their new housemates as anything but potential meals. Even though some cats are not big hunters and would rather enjoy bowls of hand-delivered kibble, don't take the chance that the activity of the bird or mice might trigger an instinctive predatory response.

Even if your cats seem uninterested in the bird or the mice, never leave them unsupervised together. If no one in your merged family is available, make sure that the bird and mice are safely in their cages out of paw's reach. You don't want a case of feline "fowl" play or a mouse murder in the house.

It is important, however, that you convey to your cats that the bird and mice are part of the family. Pay attention to signals from your cats that they are feeling more aggressive than amused by the smaller critters. Prey-focused cats tend to display overt curiosity, sit very still and stare fixedly at the prey, or twitch their tails slightly and fold their ears back. Another big clue: predators don't vocalize before they stalk and kill. However, many cats do make a distinctive chirping or cackling sound when they become aroused at the sight of birds.

It is important to reward polite, acceptable behavior in your cats by praising them and offering them small treats when they are relaxed around the bird and mice. If one of your cats displays unwanted behavior, such as pawing at the birdcage or pacing around the mice container, you can toss a small pillow or squirt water near your cat to startle and distract him (don't actually hit him!). The message you want to deliver is that unpleasant things happen when he paws or stares at the caged critters.

Although I am not a big fan of remote punishment, I am in favor of keeping birds safe. You can't erase the predatory nature in your cat, so if you wish to have a household filled with wings and fur, take extra precautions to keep mice and birds safely out of a curious cat's reach. Make sure your cat can't jump on top of the cage or perch nearby and poke a paw through the bars.

Many pets of different origins do get along, or at least tolerate one another. Some cats — especially those raised from kittenhood with birds or mice — can tone down their predatory nature and be friends. But you'll be a better friend to all your pets by keeping a close eye on their actions.

## TRUE OR FALSE?

Some common feline "facts" are actually fiction:

CATS EAT GRASS WHEN THEY ARE SICK.
Cats do not necessarily eat grass because they have upset stomachs and need to vomit. Some actually like the taste and texture. Grass provides fiber to help work out hairballs and adds vitamins such as folic acid not found in meat.

A FAT CAT IS A HAPPY CAT. Overweight cats are at risk for a host of health problems, such as diabetes, liver problems, and arthritis. Keeping your cat at her ideal weight increases the chance that she will live a long, healthy life.

MILK IS A HEALTHY TREAT FOR CATS. After kittens are weaned, their levels of lactase (the enzyme that helps with lactose digestion) drop by nearly 90 percent. That explains why many adult cats vomit or suffer from diarrhea if they ingest too much cow's milk. A spoonful or two every once in a while probably won't hurt, but milk isn't a necessary part of the feline diet. A better choice is a tablespoon of plain yogurt.

# PART II

# Chatting with Your Cat

**It is easy for us** humans to congratulate ourselves for being the world's best communicators because of our ability to talk. Some people speak several languages. Others wow us by delivering motivational speeches. But here's a reality check: our cats "speak" much more clearly than we do.

Cats are straight talkers. They put the *c* in candor. They never deceive or pretend. If they feel threatened or angered, they hiss. If they are content, they purr. In cat-to-cat chat, there is rarely a communication miscue. The message is delivered clearly through body postures and a variety of vocalizations.

But between humans and cats, breakdowns in communication occur often. What we may see as an act of defiance, like using the bathroom rug as a litter box, could be a call for help with a medical problem. We can't understand why cats flee from our hugs but often seem to seek out visitors with allergies. We don't always know the difference between "mew" and "meow."

We can communicate better with our cats by learning some feline "language." Along the way, we may commit a feline faux "paw" or two, but that's all right.

# Talk, Talk, Talk

**Q** My cat Maddie is extremely talkative. As soon as I get up in the morning, she starts meowing at me. If I "meow" back, she will answer me for as long as I am willing to play this game. My other cat, Whisper, is aptly named; he is very quiet and rarely talks to me. Why are some cats so talkative and others not?

**A** Quite simply, some cats have more to say than others. Cats are a lot like people. There are the chatty types and the ones who prefer to listen more than to talk. You didn't mention whether Maddie is a purebred or mixed, but some breeds are more prone to talking. Topping that list is the Siamese. Other Oriental breeds are also known to speak out more than quieter breeds such as Persians or Maine Coons. Of course, there are always exceptions to this rule. I've known some Siamese who seem to operate with the mute button on and some pushy Persians who never seem to stop talking until they reach the food bowl or their bed.

Cats are quick studies. They realize we are only human and that we are often oblivious to their obvious body language. They make a range of pure and complex sounds with different meanings, and they often attempt to communicate with us vocally.

It sounds as though you enjoy your chat sessions with Maddie, so I recommend using those times to reinforce your special bond. Even if she doesn't understand explicitly what you are saying, she will welcome your friendly tones and the one-on-one attention. Behavior research conducted at the University of Bristol in England has shown that people who imitate their cats' playfulness enjoy better relationships with their cats. In addition, cats who are played with tend to be more outgoing, easy natured, and better socialized.

At the end of each day, it's not the words you speak that matter so much as it is your tone of voice and your willingness to spend quality time with Maddie. But don't ignore Whisper — just because he doesn't speak up doesn't mean he won't appreciate your attention and affection!

## Can't Stay Away

**Q** My two cats often avoid visitors who want to pet them but will always march right over to my friend who has terrible allergies! Why do cats seem to make a beeline for the one person who wants to stay away from them?

**A** While some people — and dogs — enjoy being rushed by admirers, cats exhibit their own brand of class. Anything that moves quickly toward them is likely to be regarded as a threat. So even if your Aunt Lilly simply adores your Persian and wants to smother her in lipstick-coated kisses, your kitty wants no part of such overwhelming attention and flees the scene.

Cats like to call the shots and control introductions. It is safer that way, not to mention more dignified. Your friend with the allergies is doing his best to avoid making eye contact with or physically touching your cats. In cat communication, he is showing good feline manners. Your friend mistakenly thinks ignoring your cats will make them not interested, but it has the opposite effect. They regard him as non-threatening and friendly.

Silly as it sounds, ask your friend with the allergies to clap his hands and wave his arms when your cats approach him. You don't want to terrify your cats, but these gestures may be just unwelcoming enough for them to decide to keep their distance.

The easiest solution is probably to put your cats in another room and keep the door closed during your friend's visit. Make sure that room offers cat amenities like a litter box, water and food bowls, comfy bed, a toy or two, and a great perch to do some "nosy neighbor" watching of outside activities.

With your cat-admiring friends, suggest they enter the room quietly, act like a log, and not budge off the sofa for a few minutes. They should not reach for or make eye contact with your cats. With quieter body language, they may achieve the desired interaction with your two cats.

# The Purpose of Purring

**Q** My cat, Felix, loves to purr and does it quite loudly. All I have to do is pet him and he starts rumbling away. But my sister's cat, Ginger, hardly ever purrs, even though she seems to be happy and is quite pampered. I've heard a lot of different things about why cats purr. What's the real story?

**A** The phenomenon of purring has fascinated humans for ages. A lot of research has been conducted to figure out this feline mystique, but no one knows for certain why cats purr, though it is believed to be a voluntary act initiated by the central nervous system. In other words, cats purr on purpose, not just as an instinctive response.

Scientists report that cats produce purring sounds by using the diaphragm to push air back and forth across vibrating nerves in the larynx. Purring occurs in a frequency range between 25 and 150 hertz. At the lower end of the range, that rumbling sound can resemble an idling diesel engine, which has a similar velocity.

All domestic cats and most wild felids are born with the ability to purr. Cats, from young kittens to senior citizens, purr when they are happy, such as when they are being petted, anticipating dinner, or snuggling on a warm, cozy bed. Mother cats purr when nursing their kittens, and kittens purr when nursing.

> **FELINE FACT**
>
> **Did you know that cats can purr while inhaling and exhaling? That's a feat we can't imitate. Try making a purr sound as you inhale and as you exhale. It is tougher than trying to say "toy boat" 10 times fast.**

But many cats also purr when they are afraid or in pain. That helps explain why females may purr during labor and why some cats purr when they are being examined at a veterinary clinic or when they are recovering from an injury. The purring might serve to reassure or comfort the frightened cat, and some studies suggest that the low-level vibrations of purring physically stimulate feline muscles and bones to keep them healthy and actually hasten the healing process. Cats purr right to the end — when my beloved Samantha had to be euthanized due to liver disease several years ago, the sound of her purring comforted both of us as she slipped peacefully away in my arms.

## CAT CHAT DECIPHERED

Whether your cat is a fast-talking feline or a quiet kitty, you have probably noticed that she has a wide range of vocalizations. You may be surprised to learn that cats are capable of making about 30 sounds, including at least 19 variations on the simple meow. Here are some of the most common feline sounds:

**MEW.** This pleasant, high-pitched sound is used to prompt people to do a cat's bidding, as in "Please refill the food bowl" or "I'd like to go outside." Kittens make this sound to their mothers when they want to nurse.

**MEOW.** Your cat evokes this long, urgent-sounding tone to make demands and convey displeasure. The *me* signals to the owner where the cat is and the *ow* proclaims, "Look out for me." A meow might register disdain at overly vigorous petting or indicate irritation when a polite *mew* at the backdoor has been ignored.

**CHIRP.** This musical trill comes from the throat and ends in a question mark inflection. Momma cats use it to gather their kittens at nursing time. Directed to a favorite person, this sound might mean, "I'm glad you're home" or "Oh, there you are."

**CACKLE.** Highly aroused cats often emit this *ka-ka-ka* noise when they spot a bird through the window. Notice that your cat's lower jaw quivers as he cackles. It is a sound of frustration.

**MOAN.** This elongated wail of panic or protest comes from a cat who is extremely unhappy or in pain. Some cats moan when they are about to regurgitate a hairball or during a veterinary exam.

**HISS.** Plain and simple, this sound tells you to back off. It is an early warning sign before a cat defends himself by nipping or swatting. An especially furious cat will make a spitting sound as well.

**YOWL.** Angry, agitated cats will often erupt into a screaming match if they feel threatened enough to attack. These screeches often precede or accompany actual physical contact. In a non-fight situation, a disoriented senile cat might yowl, as might a deaf cat who can't hear himself. A cat might yowl in mourning after the death or departure of a companion cat. And female cats in heat will yowl incessantly, which is another good reason for spaying!

# The Healing Power of Purring

**Q** When Groucho, my big tabby, sits in my lap and starts to purr contently, I feel the stress from my day melt away. I'm sure that stroking his soft fur and listening to his purring is good for my health, but is there any scientific proof of this?

**A** Never underestimate the power of purring — scientists certainly respect that magical motoring sound. Recent studies have validated that hanging around a contented, purring cat can drop a human's high blood pressure to within normal range, decrease stress, conquer feelings of loneliness, and even bolster self-confidence. About 65 percent of American households have pets, but we are just realizing the power our pets possess in helping us to heal emotionally, physically, and mentally. Scientists are also discovering that cats and other cherished pets possess special healing powers that help people fight disease and cope with chronic conditions.

In his book *The Healing Power of Pets,* veterinarian Marty Becker describes the biochemical impact pets have on their owners' body chemistry. He interviewed numerous medical experts who provided the results of many scientific studies that support a biological basis for what we've felt intuitively — that people can be healthier by interacting positively and sharing their lives with pets. For example, the mere act of petting your cat can lower your blood pressure.

Dr. Allen Schoen, director of the Veterinary Institute for Therapeutic Alternatives in Sherman, Connecticut, has devoted his career to studying how animals can transform and improve our lives. He explains that a cat's purr stimulates our auditory nerves and provides us with a peaceful respite from the mechanical noises that are constantly bombarding our senses.

Some medical doctors even recommend "pet prescriptions" to their patients who live alone and need companionship. That's because physicians have discovered that a family pet can actually motivate some patients to give their best effort when dealing with serious illnesses such as cancer. Having a pet to care for and feed can stimulate ailing individuals to take better care of themselves.

Here are three easy and healthy ways to tap into the healing power of your feline companion:

◆ Spend some time each day just looking at, listening to, and talking with your cat. This helps release those "feel-good" biochemicals that help you relax.

◆ Rub your cat the right way. Learn to give your pet a therapeutic massage, for some one-on-one time that will soothe both of you.

◆ Engage in purposeful play with your cat and you might discover that you can let go of daily stress more easily, breathe more deeply, and laugh more freely.

# Tail as a Mood Barometer

**Q** My cat, Mimi, often holds her tail straight up in the air when she walks around our house. If she's out in the yard and she sees me come outside, her tail pops up like that, too. With dogs, I know that a relaxed, wagging tail usually means they are happy and excited. But when it comes to cats, I'm not sure how to interpret their tail signals. Do cats use their tails in the way dogs do to communicate?

**A** The versatile feline tail definitely does more than act as a rudder and provide balance. Like dogs, cats use their tails to signal their moods, sort of like those mood rings in the 1970s. Remember those? They would supposedly change colors when you were happy or angry. The key difference here is that a cat's tail position is far more reliable than those mood rings were. Recognizing the messages delivered in tail talk can help you better communicate with your cat. Here are some key tail positions and what they mean.

**HOISTED HIGH.** A confident, contented cat will hold her tail high in the air as she moves about her territory. A tail that is erect like a flagpole signals a happy mood or a friendly greeting. Cats often send this message as they approach a welcoming person. If the top third of the tail twitches as the cat nears you, this means that he totally adores you.

**QUESTION MARK.** A tail looking bent in a question mark often conveys a playful mood. This would be a good time to engage in a five- or ten-minute play session.

**FLYING LOW.** A tail positioned straight down, parallel to the legs, may represent an aggressive mood. Be wary. That said, there are exceptions to this rule. Some breeds, such as Persians, Exotics, and Scottish Folds, normally tend to carry their tails lower than their backs.

**TUCKED AWAY.** A tail curved beneath the body signals fear or submission. Something is making that cat nervous.

**PUFFED UP.** A pipe cleaner of a tail reflects a severely agitated and frightened cat who is trying to look bigger to ward off danger.

**WHIPPING.** A tail that whips rapidly back and forth indicates both fear and aggression. It is a warning that says "stay away."

**SWISHING.** A tail that swishes slowly from side to side usually means the cat is focused on an object. Cats often swish their tails right before they pounce on a toy mouse. It is part of their predatory positioning.

**TWITCHING.** A tail that twitches just at the tip is a sign of curiosity and excitement.

**CAT-TO-CAT.** A tail wrapped around another cat is equivalent to a person casually putting her arm around a favorite pal. It conveys feline friendship. My cats Callie and Little Guy often stroll down my hallway with their tails touching.

# The Halloween Pose

**Q** Occasionally, my young cat will arch his back, puff out his hair, and bounce around the room on stiff legs. He looks ridiculous. I have to laugh when he strikes that classic Halloween cat spooky pose. Why does he do that?

**A** Faced with a fight-or-flight predicament, a cat needs to deal with what he perceives to be a fearful situation. Inside your frightened cat, biochemicals are at work. Adrenaline starts coursing through his body, causing his hair to bristle, his back to arch, and his tail to puff out. The result? He looks like a poster child for Halloween symbols.

Cats strike this pose to look physically bigger and more menacing to approaching threats. Notice that your cat also turns his body sideways toward the attacker to further magnify his appearance. Outwardly, the cat looks mean and ready to rumble, but inside, he is hoping that the attacker (be it a strange dog, an unfamiliar house guest, or a startling sound on the television) will just go away and leave him alone.

This is a classic feline bluff posture. It may look comical to us, but to our cats, the threat is real and the pose is an instinctive reaction. If this posture doesn't work, the cat faces two options: flee the scene or prepare to fight.

# Seeing Eye to Eye

**Q** My cat, Daphne, has beautiful, big, round, golden eyes. She is a Bengal who I adopted as a kitten about three years ago. She has developed into a very affectionate cat who likes to play and who follows me from room to room. Sometimes I try to engage in staring contests with her for fun. I thought that cats could outstare us, but she always seems to break her stare and starts blinking at me. What is she trying to tell me?

**A** Ah, you are the proud recipient of the feline eyewink. Cats who gently flutter their eyes at selected people are conveying not only affection but also trust. Daphne is telling you in candid cat language that she adores you. Make Daphne's day by responding with soft winks back to her. She may be wowed by your cat savvy and display other forms of friendship toward you.

As for staring contests, cats save that intense look for when they are on alert or are feeling animosity toward someone or some situation, so it's best to avoid looking your cat directly in the eyes if you want to keep those happy feelings.

---

# Cat-to-Cat Communication

**Q** My four cats get along pretty well, as far as I can tell. They don't have bloody fights or nasty howling exchanges. They are all adults, ranging from three to ten years old. Each arrived at a different time. How can I tell if they like each other or simply tolerate one another?

**A** In spite of the variety of sounds described on page 68, cats rely less on sounds and more on body postures and scent marking when communicating with each other. However, some cats hiss at a feline housemate when feeling defensive or threatened.

Cats are generally thought of as solitary creatures who enjoy company only when mating or mothering, yet many cats do form close friendships. Why? That is a complex question still being studied by animal behaviorists. What is known is that space matters between cats. I'm talking about the physical space between two cats who share the same home.

Cats who at least tolerate and at best like one another require far less physical separation in a home than do feuding housemates. In addition to feline elbowroom, the availability of resources also plays a role in keeping the peace. If there is plenty of chow available for all, there is less chance of fighting over food. The same goes for the number of available litter boxes. The rule is one litter box per cat plus one.

Not all cats will cuddle up together or play together, but that doesn't mean they aren't content to share a house. Don't worry if your cats ignore each other or only sniff noses occasionally. Do be alert to signs of stress such as flattened ears, dilated pupils, hissing, and lowered tails. From your description, I'm betting that your foursome more often display relaxed postures with their ears and tails and that they all feel safe, secure, and well fed. No need to compete when all four are being pampered.

## KITTEN-GARTEN

Puppy classes are well known, but until recently, such classes were unheard of for kittens. The first ones were started about a decade ago in Australia by veterinary behaviorist Kersti Seksel.

Kitten kindergarten features two goals: socializing the kittens and helping people better understand the feline mind. The kittens learn to be handled, groomed, and examined, and to explore new places with confidence. Some kittens play with each other, while others prefer to hang out with the people handing out treats.

The ideal time to enroll is when your kitten is between twelve and sixteen weeks of age — the heart of a young feline's socialization period.

Kitten kindergarten, however, is not without controversy. Some feline experts say that these socialization classes are best suited for orphaned kittens or shelter kittens rather than kittens who have experienced normal kittenhood and learned feline rules from their mothers and siblings.

# **Dark Clothes, White Cat**

**Q** Every time I put on a pair of dark-colored dress slacks, I can count on my white cat, Toby, to enter the room and start rubbing against my legs. In no time, my slacks are covered in white hair from the knee down. I try gently pushing him away, but he persists. Why does he do this and what can I do to stop him?

**A** When a cat rubs against your leg or brushes his cheekbone against your hand, he is broadcasting two signals. The first is a form of feline flattery. You are the lucky recipient of his affection. I know, flattery will get you nowhere, except, in this case, to the place where you stash the rolling tape to remove Toby's hairy signature from your dress slacks.

The second signal is all about turf protection. Cats have scent glands on their lips, chins, forehead, and tail. We can't smell the oily residue that is deposited from these glands, but other cats (and dogs) certainly can. When Toby rubs against your legs, he is alerting other critters to back off and respect "his" property.

By gently pushing Toby, you are unwittingly reinforcing his behavior. As you shoo him away from your legs, he enjoys the touch of your hand as well as leaving his business card on your slacks. Double victory!

It's clear that you treat Toby well and that he loves you. Perhaps a little compromise is in order. Create a bit of

"Toby time" each day during which you give him some extra affection and sweet talk. Groom him regularly to remove some of his excess hair. Here's a grooming trick: run your damp hand gently against the direction your cat's coat. This removes dead hairs better than combing. You not only remove dead hairs (the only ones that cats shed), but also stimulate new hair growth. A full bath or even a dry shampoo once in a while will also help keep the amount of loose hair more manageable.

If Toby is overly insistent on rubbing against your legs, you might consider making your clothes less inviting. Lightly spray your pants with a cat-repellant spray or citronella (read the directions first to make sure they will not harm the fabric). One sniff and Toby will head the other way while you head out the door with clean clothes. But don't expect Toby to learn that it's okay to rub against your jeans but not your dress pants — you either have to accept a few hairs or discourage this display of affection entirely.

# Bounce and Pounce

 My five-month-old kitten, Rex, often goes up to our old hound dog, Gus, and starts bouncing sideways. Gus looks at Rex like he just arrived from another planet. He does his best to ignore Rex, but Rex persists. He sometimes even paws at Gus's nose and then races away. What is going on?

**A** Rex is extending an invitation to play. Kittens often arch their backs, puff up their tails (with the tips pointed down), and do this sideways disco dance to pretend that they are being spooked. Obviously, Rex is in no real danger with Gus, but he may be in danger of being bored. He wants Gus to join in a friendly game of tag.

Rex clearly needs more interactive play. Old Gus is a no-go, so I encourage you and the rest of your family to toss paper wads down hallways for Rex to pounce on or to drag a string for him to chase. He might like a game of laser tag on a wall. Just make sure that the area is free of breakable objects like your Aunt Dottie's antique vase. Also be aware

of heavy furniture that could cause injury to a fast-moving, high-jumping kitten in full-throttle play mode. Even the most agile of kittens can misjudge and slam into an immobile piece of furniture. Ouch!

Rex sounds like a delight and he deserves playmates willing to join him in some daily feline fun.

---

# Dealing with Deafness

**Q** I recently adopted Lizzy, a five-month-old white kitten with blue eyes, from a local shelter. At her first checkup, the veterinarian informed me that Lizzy is deaf. Of course I plan to keep her, but how do I communicate with a deaf cat?

**A** Lizzy is one lucky kitty to have you as her caretaker. Deaf cats do possess some added challenges, but that just makes them more special.

Some cats are born deaf. A very brief lesson on genetics: Deafness is associated with the simple autosomal dominant white gene, especially in combination with blue eyes. The chance for deafness in white, blue-eyed kittens increases dramatically when both parents are white. What about Siamese cats, you may ask? Though famous for their blue eyes, they are not born deaf because they do not have the dominant white gene.

Cats like Lizzy with white fur and two blue eyes are genetically more prone to deafness due to degeneration of the cochlear duct inside the ear. The mechanism responsible for pigmentation in the eyes also controls auditory development. When the pigment cells responsible for color are prematurely stopped, hearing is affected.

Other cats become deaf due to severe ear infections, drug toxicity, or head trauma. Old age is another cause. Whatever the cause, deaf cats are often easily startled, especially if you approach them from behind or nudge them while they are sleeping. Some deaf cats are quite vocal because they cannot hear their own voices and control the volume of their meows.

It should go without saying that for safety reasons, deaf cats need to live strictly indoors. I recommend that you make an appointment with your veterinarian to microchip Lizzy, and put an address tag on her collar indicating that she is deaf just in case someone does find her outdoors. Attach a bell to her collar so you can keep tabs on her movements.

Since Lizzy can't hear you, you need to approach her face first so as not to startle her; otherwise she might take a swipe at you out of fear. Approaching her directly prepares her for interaction. Don't forget to ask your houseguests to do the same. If you need to wake her, stomp the floor near her so she can feel the vibrations. If she is sleeping on a cat bed or piece of furniture, push on the surface next to her rather than touching her.

You can teach a deaf cat to come, sit, and perform other tricks using hand signals. You can also communicate by using a flashlight or laser pointer. Use the flashing light to guide your cat where you wish her to go. Flashing lights can also be employed to distract a deaf cat who may be on a kitchen counter, clawing the couch, or committing another feline misdeed.

The bottom line is that with help, deaf cats can enjoy full, robust lives. They are remarkably adaptable and will compensate by relying more on their other senses, such as sight and smell.

# Talking to Cats

**Q** When I say the word "treat," my cat, Toto, comes running. If I say "walk," he heads for the door where I keep his leash and harness. He loves taking short walks outside. Can cats understand words the way dogs can?

**A** Just like dogs, cats are more masterful at interpreting voice tones and body language than learning the actual words. They constantly size up our spoken syllables and gestures to determine if we are delivering praise or dishing out discipline. Even without words, they pick up our emotions and intentions.

Here's a catty challenge for you. Without making any body gestures, make eye contact with Toto and in a stern voice say, "What a good kitty you are. Let me give you some catnip." Then make eye contact and say in a cheery tone, "You are such a bad kitty. I hate when you scratch the furniture." My money is on Toto being more apt to approach you when you speak in a happy voice than when you speak in a harsh, scolding tone.

This exercise demonstrates that it is usually not what you say, but how you say it that counts for your cat. Even though we speak different languages, our savvy felines pay attention to our expressions and our habits. Some quickly associate the sound of their names with their owners wanting their attention.

My cat Callie goes to the screen door off my upstairs balcony when I say, "Callie, do you want to go outside?" Of course, as I am saying that sentence, I am also heading toward the balcony with my hand outstretched to open the door. If I make the same gestures and maintain my happy voice but change the words to: "Hey Callie, do you want to go surfing?" Callie happily follows me to the balcony door to get some supervised fresh air — without a worry of getting a single drop of the mighty ocean on her coat.

## COLORFUL CHARACTERS

Joan Miller, all-breed Cat Fanciers' Association judge, is an expert on feline personality traits. While there is no scientific evidence to validate why cats with orange in their coats can act a little "nuts" compared to their solid black littermates, many cat lovers agree that calicos, tortoiseshells, and female red tabbies often display extra feistiness and spunk.

Miller reports that a "theory of the orange gene" is somehow connected to personality traits. She points out that the Cheshire Cat in the children's classic *Alice in Wonderland* was a red tabby. And we know how nuts he was!

The orange gene is sex-linked (X) and not on the same chromosome as all the other color genes. Therefore it is possible only for female cats, because they have two X genes, to have black and orange coat colors at the same time. Males, with their XY chromosomes, can be black or orange, but not both. This means that calico and tortoiseshell cats are always female — and female cats are often not as mellow as males anyway.

# Hands Off My Belly!

**Q** Alexis, my one-year-old calico, doesn't mind when I scratch under her chin, or give her head pets, but she definitely does not like me to rub her belly. I've had other cats and dogs who seem to beg to have their bellies rubbed. Why doesn't she like her belly touched?

**A** I am not sure how long you have had Alexis, but calicos tend to be a bit apprehensive and cautious, especially in their earlier years. A veterinarian friend once told me, "Calicos are a lot like chocolate. Sweet on the outside and nuts on the inside." He said it in jest, but it carried some meaning. Whatever color the cat, however, the belly is one of the most vulnerable places on a cat's body, and many cats are wary of exposing this soft spot.

All felines need to become accustomed to being handled by people. Trust must be cultivated. For now, respect your cat's wishes and avoid belly rubs. Give her some time to become used to being handled by you and to learn that you won't foist unwanted attention on her. If Alexis strikes a belly-up pose and appears relaxed next to you, praise her, but don't touch her belly until you're sure she is inviting you to do so.

Instead, treat Alexis to some purposeful touch like massaging up and down her spine, using your finger and thumb (not your nails). Build up her confidence in you by petting her on her head and under her chin and welcoming her on your lap or by your side when you read or watch television.

Alexis may come around and turn into a cuddly love bug who will request that you shower her with friendly petting, even on her belly. If not, just understand that some cats have certain areas where they don't like being touched.

---

# Howling and Yowling

**Q** I have two Siamese cats, a neutered male named Kai and a spayed female named Kiki. Both are about six years old from the same litter. Kiki behaves well, but not Kai. As soon as the sun goes down, Kai starts pacing the house and howling as loud as he can. I've tried quieting him by giving him attention when he seems upset, but no matter what I do, he keeps howling. I'm having trouble sleeping. How can I quiet him down?

**A** Cats are naturally crepuscular, which means that they sleep a lot during the day and become more active at dusk and dawn. When the sun goes down, Kai has plenty of energy and he starts to pace and vocalize, perhaps out of frustration that he cannot join in various feline activities occurring outside.

Since his howling has escalated to the point that it has become a serious issue, the first step is to determine what is causing this hypervocalization in Kai. You may be able to blame genetics. After all, Siamese are predisposed to being big talkers. Increased howling may also be linked to Kai's need for attention or it might have a medical cause. I advise you to have him examined by your veterinarian to rule out any hidden injury or illness causing him pain. Some cats become very vocal when they develop hyperthyroidism.

The cause of the yowling may be an emotional issue, such as anxiety or fear. Work with your veterinarian on selecting appropriate treatments or medications that can address these medical or emotional causes.

If you determine that his howling is just a demand for attention, you can extinguish his behavior by purposely ignoring his high-volume vocals. This won't be easy; initially Kai will probably howl louder and more frequently when he discovers that you are not responding. When he starts up, do not say anything — resist the temptation to tell him to quiet down. Just leave the room or shut the door so that he can't see you.

At night, keep him out of your room and do not give even the slightest response, even to tell him to quiet down. You can start cueing him that you plan to ignore him by making a special sound like a duck cluck as you leave the room. This is known as a bridging stimulus and is used to alert a cat that the owner is about to withdraw attention. The key is to be patient and to avoid punishment. After all, any attention, including scolding, is still attention in the mind of Kai.

Another step is to tweak his feeding and sleeping schedules. If possible, play with him more during the day, which will cut down on his daytime napping and make him more tired at night. Provide his biggest meal at night, right before bedtime. A cat with a full belly is more apt to sleep than be active.

In some cases, a howling cat will settle down if tucked into a comfy crate at bedtime. (It has to be large enough to include a litter box, with some room between it and the sleeping area.) This tactic does not work with all cats because they are not den animals like dogs, but some cats do seem to like having a cozy bedroom of their own. Just make sure that you make this a welcoming place with plush bedding and maybe a treat or a pinch of catnip, and not a place of banishment.

# Case of Nip and Run

**Q** My cat, Peaches, is a Siamese mix. She loves to cuddle with me, but sometimes when I am petting her, she bites me. Occasionally it is hard enough to break the skin. Why does she bite, and can I train her not to bite after 12 years of living with me?

**A** Peaches is biting the hand that feeds her, and without any apologies. It is easy to mistake the reason behind the nip. Peaches is not delivering a love bite, but rather a clear indication that she has endured enough of human kindness. Her nip translates into "Kindly stop petting me or I will bite harder."

Some cats bite because as kittens they were permitted to play "hand wrestling" with their owners, who considered it cute antics. They grow up thinking it is okay to bite and swat at hands.  But when they do it as adults with big teeth and sharp claws, they aren't nearly as cute.

Other cats bite because they are scared or do not feel well, but because this has been going on her whole life, it sounds like a classic case of petting-induced aggression. While some cats can tolerate being petted, others feel overstimulated by the sensation and automatically react by lashing out. Peaches is probably lashing out at you as a last resort after delivering what she believes to be clear pre-strike warnings. These may include tail lashing, ear flicking, dilated pupils, shifting position, tensing muscles, and ceasing to purr. When Peaches displays these warning signals, that's your cue to stop petting. She has communicated to you in her best cat way that she is done with being petted.

Do not be so eager to pet Peaches for a while. Greet her in a friendly tone, but avoid petting her for a couple of days. This will make her desire your physical attention. When you do pet her, do so for just a few seconds and then stop. By being better in tune with her body signals, you can stop before Peaches feels overwhelmed and save your hand from an unwanted bite.

# Beating Up the Poor Dog

**Q** I never thought I would live to see the day that a cat would bully a dog. But unfortunately, that's the case in my household. My three-year-old tabby, Roo, taunts, stalks, and even swipes at my dog, Tigger. Tigger is a two-year-old male toy poodle-terrier mix who weighs about the same as the cat. Why does Roo badger Tigger, and what can I do to stop this behavior? I'm afraid Roo will injure Tigger.

**A** The real truth about cats and dogs is that dogs are not always the bullies. Some cats torment their canine roommates. It isn't about physical size; it's all about attitude. I've seen a cat take on a German shepherd and send that big dog fleeing in fear. Bully cats like Roo want to control practically every situation. They may even attempt to push their people around, too, by demanding meals when they want them and nipping hands when they have decided they have received enough petting.

Bully cats do not accept punishment or corrections, but they do have a weak spot — they want attention. Use that to your advantage to help Tigger. Retraining a bossy feline is much like training a dominant dog. Start by exercising Roo more frequently to expend some of his excessive energy and turn his attention to you as a playmate instead of poor Tigger. Protect your hands by engaging him in games with a fishing pole toy or cat teaser (a coiled wire with a small bundle of lightweight wood on one end that moves erratically, imitating the movement of a butterfly).

With regard to Tigger, the first step is to stop the attack. Look for early warning signs and stop a fight before it starts. Right before an attack, a cat will typically dip his head, arch his back end, and shimmy a bit. If you see this, try to remain calm. Scolding and high-pitched shrieks may only serve to fuel Roo's aggressiveness toward Tigger. Instead, step in and try distracting Roo with food treats or a favorite toy or spend a moment rubbing under his chin. Cats can't be happy and mad at the same time.

Separate the two when you cannot be around to supervise them. Avoid having them together during high-energy times, like at mealtimes and when you arrive home. Reintroduce them when they are both tired — for instance, after you have played with Roo and taken Tigger for a brisk walk. When you do bring them together, keep Tigger on a leash and let him learn Roo's signals. Do this until you see that both pets are calm. Then unleash Tigger. Finally, make sure that Roo's claws are trimmed to avoid injuries to Tigger.

## Feuding Felines

**Q** I have two cats under two years old who are not related. I adopted Abby first and brought home Buster two months later. Within the first day, they were buddies. But last week, Abby's attitude toward Buster turned hostile. I am now keeping them in different parts of the house. When the door is accidentally opened, Abby will try to attack Buster who hisses and runs away to hide. I love both cats dearly and wish they could be friends again. What can I do to restore the peace?

**A** Cats are pros at hiding pain and discomfort. An underlying medical condition may be the cause of Abby's sudden temper outbursts, so my first piece of advice is that you have her examined by your veterinarian. It is not unusual, however, for cats who have coexisted peacefully to suddenly begin spatting. Try to pinpoint when Abby's behavior changed. This may be a case of redirected aggression.

Sometimes an indoor cat becomes upset or angry at the sight of a cat or other critter outside the window. Feeling frustrated, or perhaps threatened, the indoor cat will unleash her hostility on the closest target — usually another cat in the house. Or one cat will return from a veterinary visit and smell peculiar to her feline housemate who then responds by hissing or attacking this suddenly strange intruder.

Inside the home, cats tend to use a "time-sharing" approach for favorite locations. One cat may claim the sofa in the morning while a second cat takes over that spot in the afternoon. Some homes turn into combat zones when there is a change in routine or when one cat or both feel the need to defend their timed turf.

You are taking the correct initial steps by separating Abby and Buster for their own safety and to reduce stress levels. Each cat should have access to all the feline amenities they deserve. That list includes: a window for viewing, litter box, food, water, treats, toys, and bedding. Every day, switch places, but leave their food bowls and litter boxes.

These tactics get them used to the idea of living together and sharing places and objects.

When you visit each cat, take a slightly damp washcloth and rub it over Abby's back, then on Buster, and back on Abby to share their scents. The goal is to swap scents with the hope that they become more accepting of each other. While this is a common technique used to introduce two cats for the first time, it is also effective to get resident cats who are starting to feud to become reacquainted on friendlier, or at least tolerant, terms.

After several days, reintroduce them by cracking open the door to let them see one another but not be able to touch one another. After another few days, put a screen or tall baby gate in the doorway so that they can see one another more fully. If all goes well, confine the cats in a room, but place one of them in a crate and let the other roam freely. Then switch places.

If both continue to behave, you can gradually allow them to be in the house together. After any outbursts, however, go back a step or two to reinforce success. Reuniting Abby and Buster may take some time, so please be patient as you strive to restore peace. In extreme cases, you may need to consult a veterinarian about temporarily using mood-altering medications to decrease the aggression in Abby and the fear in Buster.

My parting advice is that you resist the temptation to coddle Buster or to shout at Abby. You may unintentionally reinforce his fear and her aggression.

# The Dreaded Doorbell

**Q** My two-year-old cat, Sugar, has always been a scaredy-cat. When our doorbell rings, she races out of sight. I'll find her under my bed or even under my bedspread. When I try to introduce her to visiting friends, Sugar tries desperately to wiggle out of my arms. She has even scratched my arms trying to escape. Why is she so scared and what can I do to calm her down?

**A** My cat Callie pulled a disappearing act when guests arrived for the first four years of her life. Some of my friends didn't believe she existed! Like Callie, Sugar is exhibiting avoidance behavior in response to anything new in her environment, especially people. What causes some cats to be fearful while their littermates are outgoing is not known, but animal behaviorists identify several possible reasons.

**GENETIC PREDISPOSITION.** Some cats seem to be born reacting to new people, places, and objects with sheer fear. Even with gentle handling and positive experiences as kittens, some cats remain shy and a little standoffish with strangers.

**EMULATING THE QUEEN'S BEHAVIOR.** Kittens form habits by copying their mother between the ages of four and eight weeks. If the mother is fearful of strangers, the kittens will learn to be afraid from her. Depending on the kitten's genetic predisposition, this initial shyness may go away with maturity and repeated good experiences with strangers.

**LACK OF SOCIALIZATION.** For kittens, the period of prime socialization to people is between two and seven weeks of age. During this time, it is important for kittens to be handled by different people in pleasant ways. Under-socialized kittens are likely to be scared of strangers and may hiss, spit, strike out, or dash away.

**TRAUMATIC EXPERIENCES.** Cats at any age can develop scaredy-cat syndrome if they are exposed to a traumatic situation such as being physically abused, lost, or attacked by a dog.

The more positive experiences you can offer Sugar with different people, places, and situations, the better she will adjust to future exposures. As you work to bolster Sugar's confidence, be patient and recognize that you will not convert your flee-minded feline into a meet-and-greet cat overnight. Focus on small but steady steps of progress, and be aware that you may never turn her into a party girl.

Since you know that visitors are the cause of her fright, recruit a couple of friends who are calm and who like cats. Ask them to come inside, sit quietly, and not seek out Sugar's attention. To keep Sugar from fleeing, put her in a room ahead of time where you can close the door and keep her from dashing away and hiding. Then, have your guests join you in the room with Sugar to watch a movie or listen to soft music. The goal is to have Sugar see them and realize they won't hurt her.

Build up positive associations for Sugar by having your guests offer treats. At first, place a bit of tasty cat food or a special kitty treat next to them so she can approach without having to interact. You want to set Sugar up for success, and it will take time to desensitize her. Eventually, Sugar will realize that these people will not pursue her or try to pick her up. She may develop the confidence to approach them and actually take a treat that is offered. Let her make the decision to come closer and stop the experiment if she reacts fearfully.

Callie was a frightened cat for her first four years. But I knew she couldn't resist treats. I had my friends leave treats on the bottom of the stairs and move away so that Callie could muster the courage to climb down and eat the treats. Now she takes treats out of their hands. Sugar may never become a lap cat to your guests, but these tips can help mitigate some of her fears and make her more comfortable in your home.

# Bella's Mute Button

**NO ONE ENJOYS A MOUTHY CAT,** especially one who howls in the middle of the night. Described as a chatty cat at the best of times, Bella turned up the volume and started to screech and wail, especially between the hours of one and seven a.m. She roamed the apartment, yowling in each room. When Bella's owner, Lori, contacted me, she was fed up with her three-year-old spayed calico and longing for a full night's sleep.

Lori and I discussed the many causes for feline hyper-vocalization, including attention seeking, pain or hunger, aggression, anxiety, fear, and medical problems. A medical exam ruled out a chronic urinary tract infection, hyperthy-roidism, or other underlying medical condition. In taking a detailed history, I discovered some clues behind Bella's bel-lowing that pointed to behavioral causes.

Bella, who was adopted as a young kitten from a shelter, had no issues with the family's other cat. In fact, she played and groomed the other cat on a regular basis. But Bella's loud talk started just about the time Lori began working full-time away from home. In Bella's case, attention seek-ing and/or anxiety were the most likely explanations for her hypervocalization.

Insistent cat chat is usually directed at owners, not other cats. Bella's yelling garnered what she wanted: Lori's atten-tion. Each time Lori responded by reprimanding Bella, she inadvertently rewarded and reinforced the behavior.

To tone down Bella, I instructed Lori to ignore her cat's vocals. I warned her that at first, Bella's feline stubbornness would kick in and she would respond by vocalizing louder and longer. Lori listened to my advice and ignored Bella's demanding yowls until Bella realized that she received no attention at all for her noisy ways.

To answer Bella's needy nature, I instructed Lori to schedule exercise and playtimes with Bella at night to tire her out. Lori also followed my other suggestions: introducing clicker training and providing Bella with a climbing cat frame or cat condo filled with toys to pounce on, stalk, and swat at. Placing a bird feeder near a window provided Bella with a perfect place to observe and kept her entertained during the day when Lori was at work.

After playtime, Lori started feeding Bella a high-quality canned-food meal right before bedtime. This was designed to change Bella's sleep–wake cycle. Well-exercised, mentally stimulated, fed-at-bedtime cats tend to be more content during the long hours of human sleeping time.

Through it all, Lori was realistic and knew not to expect overnight success. She was persistent and consistent and finally achieved her ultimate goal: sound sleep and a quieter, happier cat.

*Contributed by Alice Moon-Fanelli, certified applied animal behaviorist*

## SIGNS OF STRESS

Cats feeling stressed may exhibit any or all of the following behaviors:

◆ Excessive grooming, to the point of creating bald patches

◆ Hiding

◆ Exhibiting more aggression

◆ Eating less or more than usual

◆ Suddenly skipping the litter box or spraying in the house

◆ Indicating depression by non-responsiveness and/or excessive sleeping

# Cats and Kids

**Q** We're planning to adopt a cat soon. Our kids, ages seven and ten, have been pestering us for some time to have a pet, and they promise to help take care of a cat. They have friends with cats and enjoy playing with them. What can you recommend about safely introducing a cat to kids?

**A** Growing up with a cat or any other cuddly pet certainly enhances a childhood. My first pet was a cat named Corky who joined our family when I was eight years old. Corky loved to swim in our backyard lake with our two dogs. Four decades later, I still have vivid memories of that feline pal.

To prepare for your new family member, call for a family meeting to talk about the pros and cons of adopting a cat or a kitten. Kittens put the *p* in play and the *d* in destructiveness. During their first year, they explore their environment with reckless abandon. They grow up quickly, and your cute, friendly kitten might mature into a standoffish adult. If you adopt an adult cat at a shelter, you will have a better idea of his true personality, whether affectionate or aloof. Look for cats who can tolerate busy households with the television or stereo blaring, kids running up and down hallways, and people coming and going. Stay away from shy cats who may hide or become frightened by household hubbub.

Some pedigreed breeds enjoy reputations for being children friendly. A good example is the Abyssinian. Abys thrive in a noisy household with kids and often will jump right into the action and beg for bear hugs!

Before you bring your new pet home, create a cat care schedule and post it on the refrigerator door or bulletin board. Everyone in the family should be assigned duties that can be checked off when they clean the litter box, provide fresh water, feed the cat, and groom the cat.

Educate your kids about the best ways to interact with cats. For example, cats do not like when people run up to them and smother them in bear hugs. A new cat may feel a bit unsure at first, so your children can help him feel at home by being quiet and gentle. Tell them to sit and be still and let the cat approach them. When he does, have your children hold out their hands to allow the cat to sniff and rub up against.

Alert your children not to disturb a cat who is sleeping or using a litter box. He may feel startled or trapped and react by nipping or scratching them. Show them the right way to hold a cat by placing one hand or arm under the cat's front legs and supporting the hind legs with the other hand or arm. Tell them to be respectful when a cat starts to wiggle and wants to get down.

Most cats will not tolerate being dressed up or pushed in baby strollers, but there are always exceptions. If your new cat doesn't enjoy this sort of attention, your children

need to know that there are other ways to play with their pet. Explain that they should never wrestle roughly with a cat or encourage a cat to swat and bite their fingers. Instead, have them use fishing pole–type cat toys or toss toy mice for the cat to chase and pounce.

Finally, show them the right way to pet a cat and how to brush and comb the coat. Cats usually prefer to be stroked from head to tail, not patted on the head. Gently running a damp hand against the direction of the coat, however, removes dead hair and is a good way to pet and groom at the same time. These activities will help to strengthen the friendship between your children and their new pal.

# Dealing with a Frisky Fido

**Q** Our three-year-old cats, Kate and Allie, have very different personalities. Kate is outgoing, friendly, and good-natured. Allie is timid, a bit high-strung, and affectionate with us but not with our guests. Recently, we adopted a Labrador puppy named Marley. He is about five months old and extremely interested in the cats. He watches them all the time and wants to chase them. Kate stands her ground and swats Marley on the nose. He immediately retreats. Allie, however, runs and hides when Marley approaches. How can I get Allie to stand up for herself and fight back?

**A** Cats, like people, have many different personalities. Clearly, Kate and Allie have different attitudes toward playful puppies. Kate projects confidence and is actually teaching Marley about what Aretha sings about: r-e-s-p-e-c-t. Kate is also teaching Marley some manners with a little tough love. Just make sure to trim her nails regularly because you don't want her to injure Marley with a sharp swat.

Unfortunately, those lessons are being contradicted by Allie's actions. As a result, you might have one confused pup. Allie lacks Kate's feeling of security and views this huge canine beast as a threat. Rather than stand paw to paw with him, she takes the fright-and-flee option and tries to disappear. It is not Allie's nature to stand and hold her ground.

The best time to introduce cats and dogs are when they are young. The first two or three months of life is the prime socialization period, a key time for cats and dogs to cultivate friendships. But it's not too late to work on Marley's cat-greeting skills and bolster Allie's self-confidence.

Let's start with Marley. Labs tend to be fun loving and eager to please, so you have that working in your favor. Your mission is to teach Marley two important obedience commands, *down* and *stay,* so that he remains in place even when Allie enters the room. To set him up for success, attach a long leash or clothesline to his collar to control his movement inside your home when you are around to supervise. Hold the other end or tie it to a heavy piece of furniture that can handle the muscle of a lunging Lab. When you are not home, keep Marley in a crate or in an area separated from the cats.

Keep a bag of treats handy. When Marley eyes Allie, redirect his attention by showing him a treat. Calmly instruct him to sit or down or stay. Do not yell because you will only heighten his excitement and Allie's fearfulness. If Marley ignores the commands and the treat and starts to chase Allie, step on the line to stop him. When Marley consistently demonstrates that he won't chase Allie, let him move around the house with his leash dragging behind him. If he starts to chase Allie, step on the line.

As for Allie, make sure that she has stress-free escape routes and dog-free zones. Clear out under your bed and provide a tall cat tree or wide sturdy shelves for her to perch on out of Marley's reach. If possible, install baby gates in doorways of rooms where you keep your cats' food and water bowls and litter boxes.

Let Allie run to her safe spot when she feels threatened. Do not rush after her and try to shower her with kindness or sweet talk. These tactics only backfire by mistakenly conveying to Allie that she should be worried about this big dog. Act cool and speak in an upbeat tone.

Never force the two together. Cats feel most secure when they have "four on the floor" (all four paws touching the ground). Control the contact between them and go slow. Always maintain control of Marley and let Allie enter and leave the room freely.

Some dogs and cats can form close friendships. Others tolerate one another. As long as Allie feels safe — and Marley heeds your commands — life should get less fearful for Allie.

# Harassing the Houseguests

**Q** My cat Simon is an outgoing cat who struts around like he rules the house. Although he is neutered and well behaved (at least with me), his reactions toward houseguests vary, depending on who is visiting, how long they stay, and to what extent they disrupt his routine. Sometimes he is quite friendly, and other times he is downright mean. He even peed in my uncle's open suitcase during one long visit. My other cat, Garfunkel, treats all houseguests the same. He runs and hides and tries to stay out of their sight. What can I do to ease Garfunkel's fears and make Simon treat our guests with better manners?

**A** With names like these, it's a shame there is a lack of harmony with houseguests. One of your problems may be that cats crave routines. They become accustomed to a sedate, indulged life. They usually don't enjoy surprises like the arrival of a strange-smelling person who may rudely commandeer the spare bedroom where they are accustomed to taking their afternoon naps. Too many changes, too fast, without proper planning, can trigger acute stress and unhappiness.

Even sociable cats like Simon can get annoyed or over-stimulated by houseguests. How each cat reacts depends a lot on his age, health status, temperament, personality, lifestyle, and previous experience with unfamiliar people. Some cats become upset enough to mark their territory by urinating on the belongings of guests.

One thing you can do to make visits go more smoothly is to remind your guests of all your furry roommates and describe any particular habits. For example, my 19-year-old cat is becoming somewhat senile and is partially blind, so he meows quite a lot and occasionally bumps into walls. My cats also like to sleep with my visitors, so I warn people to shut the bedroom door if they don't want company at night. I also mention a few house rules regarding my furry housemates.

◆ No sneaking them table scraps or other human food.

◆ Be careful with the outside doors — my cats live indoors only.

◆ Don't rush up to them — let them approach you first.

As for Simon and Garfunkel, plan ahead a few days, if possible, before the arrival of your guests. Slowly relocate your cat's bedding from the spare bedroom to a new safe haven that is off-limits to guests, such as your bedroom closet or a utility room or a small bathroom.

When guests arrive, strive to maintain as much of a daily routine as possible. That means cleaning out the litter boxes regularly and feeding your cats at the usual time and place. Spend at least a few minutes each day playing with your cats and devoting some time for cuddling. You may consider masking loud or unfamiliar noises (like your uncle's heavy snoring or your sister's high-pitched giggles) by playing a radio or CD player softly in your cats' safe haven space. Don't force your pets to interact with your guests.

For cats exhibiting signs of stress, you may ease anxiety with a product called Feliway. It mimics a comforting facial pheromone produced by cats and comes as a wall plug-in. This product, available at pet supply stores, diffuses the pheromones throughout a room.

If your cat does engage in inappropriate elimination or other destructive behavior, recognize that he is signaling that he is extremely stressed and feels the need to mark his territory. Do not punish him because that can only heighten his stress.

# Down on Dating

**Q** My cat, Bailey, is about six years old. I have had him since he was a kitten. He has every toy you can think of and I dote on him. He loves me, but he seems to hate my boyfriend, Nick. Whenever Nick visits, Bailey spits, growls, and hisses. If Nick tries to approach him, Bailey hisses and swats at him or dashes out of the room. This is causing problems in our relationship. I would never give up Bailey, but I really like this guy. Why doesn't my cat like my boyfriend? What can I do to get Bailey to at least tolerate Nick?

**A** Welcome to the new world of dating in which a cat has a big say in your love life. I remember a savvy senior friend named Florence who taught me a lot about dating when I was in college. I rented the upstairs of her house in Crown Point, Indiana. I lived there with my childhood cat, Corky, who was 12 at the time. Corky had the run of her entire house, and Florence would size up my boyfriends by how they treated Corky and how Corky reacted to them. She used to tell me, "If a man can't love an animal, he can't love you." She was right.

In your case, Bailey is feeling a bit threatened by this new guy commandeering so much of your time and attention. He is responding in the only way he knows — by hissing, swatting, staring, and dashing to another room. You didn't mention how your boyfriend reacts to Bailey's ill will. If he doesn't like cats, Bailey is certainly aware of that fact and reacting to these vibes.

But if this guy is willing to make your relationship work, the best strategy is to make him more popular in Bailey's eyes. Start by asking Nick to display a friendly but nonchalant attitude toward Bailey. In other words, he shouldn't try too hard to win over Bailey by forcing affection on him. Instruct him never to stare directly into Bailey's eyes or make any kind of direct approach, as cats view these as threatening signs.

The next step is to have Nick bribe Bailey with delicious, highly aromatic treats. Let your boyfriend be the only one who gives A-plus treats to Bailey so that he associates Nick with something positive.

For the third step, have Nick bring toys or engage in playing one of Bailey's favorite games while you watch from the sidelines. The two need to develop a relationship of their own. It will take time, but the payoff could be the beginning of a beautiful friendship between them.

---

# Is My Cat Senile?

**Q** My 17-year-old cat, Sammy, ambles around the house late at night, howling mournfully. Sometimes, he wanders into a room during the day and just stands there looking confused. He used to greet his favorite visitors with a happy chirping sound, but now when they come up to him, he doesn't seem to recognize them. He used to love jumping in my lap, but now I have to bend down and pick him up. Alzheimer's disease is so cruel to people; can cats develop this condition, too?

**A** On the outside, our felines often look younger than their physical years. But cats, sadly, are not immune to cognitive dysfunction. Some do indeed become senile in their senior years.

I have my senior cat (a 19-year-old who exhibits many of the behaviors you describe) examined regularly by my veterinarian, and I encourage you to do the same for Sammy to rule out any possible underlying medical condition. Hyperthyroidism, liver disease, kidney disease, and urinary tract infection are examples of diseases that may cause hypervocalization or confusion. Some cats who become deaf also start yowling frequently.

> **FELINE FACT**
> A cat's heart beats about twice as fast as a human's, at a rate of 155 times per minute.

Some cats start to exhibit certain telltale signs of cognitive dysfunction around age 12. Many animal behaviorists use the acronym DISH to refer to the symptoms and signs commonly associated with feline senility.

**D IS FOR DISORIENTATION.** Cats who are disoriented often walk aimlessly, stare at walls, get "stuck" in corners, seem to be lost in their own home, or lose their balance and fall.

**I IS FOR INTERACTIONS.** Cats with impaired mental function often display changes in their interactions with people. They're less likely to greet people when they come home or to seek out a lap, as is the case with Sammy.

**S IS FOR SLEEP.** Cats who once slept through the night may prowl restlessly, vocalizing as they roam.

**H IS FOR HOUSETRAINING.** Proper bathroom habits often go by the wayside, not for medical reasons or displeasure with the state of a litter box, but because the cat just forgets to use it.

To ease the nighttime howling, try to break his daytime sleep cycle by frequently but gently waking him during the day. Or offer Sammy pieces of turkey or lactose-free milk at bedtime. Both contain tryptophan, an amino acid shown to possess sedative properties (which explains why you feel sleepy after a big Thanksgiving dinner). The idea is to make him more tired at night. Some golden oldies will snooze through the night if you treat them to a heated cozy or pad; look for one that plugs in at very low heat and has a washable cover. If these steps do not work,

you may ask your veterinarian to prescribe an antihistamine, which can cause drowsiness.

Try to stick to a routine as much as possible for Sammy. Add some extra litter boxes in different rooms and on each level of your home. This will help cut down on any "missed" litter box opportunities. Avoid litter boxes with covers, as old cats find it harder to get into them. Lower sides are best too as the hind legs are sometimes stiff.

Most important, shower Sammy with love. Spend plenty of time cuddling him and speaking to him in reassuring tones. Enjoy the time you have left with your ageless wonder.

# Knowing When to Say Good-bye

**Q** I hate that cats don't live as long as we do. My latest cat, Ozzie, has been diagnosed with liver disease. When I first adopted him 13 years ago, he was a spirited, spunky little ball of fur. Through the years, he has grown into a kind, loving cat. I am working with my veterinarian on a treatment plan, but I know this disease moves quickly. I worry about Ozzie. I don't want him to be in any pain. How will I know when it is the right time to euthanize him?

**A** Deciding when to say good-bye to a loyal cat is certainly one of life's hardest choices. When a cat or other family pet becomes terminally ill or is critically injured, or the cost for treatment is financially beyond your means, euthanasia may be the best option.

I applaud you for working closely with your veterinarian on Ozzie's medical treatment. During one of your next appointments, make sure you discuss the specifics involved in the euthanasia procedure. You may be amazed at how peaceful and pain-free this procedure is.

Find out if your vet is willing to make a house call. You will need to decide if you want your cat's body to be buried or cremated. Think about your own needs and determine if you would prefer to be alone after the procedure or if you want to spend time with a special friend.

As for the right time, that is certainly an individual call. Let Ozzie's quality of life guide you. You will probably know when the time has come by paying careful attention to Ozzie's signals. He may stop eating, be unable to use the litter box on his own, stop grooming himself, or begin to sleep all the time. Also look for any signs of pain or discomfort that cannot be eased with medication.

Please keep this final thought in mind: The definition of euthanasia is "easy death." Being able to end physical suffering in our pets is truly the last gift we can give them.

# PART III

# Kitty Quirks and Funny Felines

**My favorite television show** when I was a child was *Kids Say the Darndest Things* with host Art Linkletter. He made his young guests feel at ease, and they responded to his questions with comments that surprised and amused viewers. At the time, I wished there was a show like that featuring cats and dogs.

After all, many strange and fun antics occurred in my childhood home thanks to our two dogs and one very amusing cat. If Crackers and Peppy weren't wowing our neighbors with their howling duets, our cat, Corky, was raising eyebrows with his habit of swimming in our backyard lake. And it wasn't just our house. One neighbor had an overweight Boston terrier who snorted instead of barking, and there was a cat with a knack for popping up inside a different garage each morning.

Face the feline facts. Cats *do* the darndest things, but they do not provide explanations. They might be puzzling and mystifying but they are never boring. In this section, I help you think more like a cat so that you can better understand and appreciate the need to knead, the attraction to water faucets, the zest for catnip, and more.

# Perplexed by Tail-chasing Cat

**Q** My cat, Peanut, an eight-year-old domestic long-hair, has what seem like major arguments with her tail. She growls and hisses at it, sometimes bites it, and occasionally runs in circles after it. She also has been grooming herself to the point that she has bald spots on her coat. If I intervene and pick her up, she gets agitated, wiggles out of my arms, and flees to another room. Do you have any ideas as to what may be causing this? What can I do to stop Peanuts from bothering her tail and pulling out hair?

**A** Tail chasing may result from physical problems causing pain or discomfort in the tail area or it, more rarely, can be a behavioral problem (and yes, a weird one at that). In either case, this is a problem that requires professional intervention. Book an appointment with your veterinarian to rule out any possible injury to the tail, infection in the anal sac area, spinal cord problem, or neurological disease before regarding this as a behavior problem.

From your description, Peanuts may be suffering from feline hyperesthesia. According to Alice Moon-Fanelli, a certified-applied animal behaviorist, this complicated condition includes some compulsive and neurological behaviors. Typically, a cat with this condition will display dilated pupils, excessive skin rippling, and frenetic self-directed grooming that results in hair loss. The cat often targets the tail and flank area with this over-the-top grooming. Some cats become vocal and aggressive and may appear to hallucinate by acting afraid of their tail, sporting an excited, manic look, and fleeing the room. These cats are extremely sensitive to touch when they are experiencing these symptoms and may lash out at people trying to restrain them.

For unknown reasons, feline hyperesthesia episodes tend to occur more often in the early morning or in the evening. Aggressive behavior may appear spontaneously and for no seemingly apparent reason. Following an episode, the poor cat will appear confused.

Initially, some owners regard such behaviors displayed by their cats as cute or eye-catching. But when the problem starts to occur more frequently and for longer duration, it becomes a cause for real concern. Work with your veterinarian or behaviorist to pinpoint the situation that may have triggered Peanut's tail chasing.

# Earlobe Lover

**Q** I have had Smokey, a two-year-old cat, since he was seven weeks old. He is very affectionate, but sometimes he insists on climbing up on me and licking my earlobes. He will even wrap his paws around my neck to get a better grip and then use his rough tongue on my earlobes — it hurts! I like cuddling with him, but I have to push him off me to make him quit. Why does he do this and what can I do to make him stop?

**A** Seven weeks is very young to be separated from the mother cat, so it might be that Smokey's behavior stems from being weaned too early. Whatever the reason, Smokey is grooming you. Keep in mind that mutual grooming is a normal behavior among feline friends. It doesn't matter if it is cat to cat, cat to dog, or in your case, cat to favorite person. Smokey adores you to the point of performing this obnoxious action. This earlobe fetish may also provide Smokey with a calming outlet.

You did not mention how long Smokey has gotten away with licking your earlobes. A lot of undesirable feline habits start in kittenhood. And a lot of those habits are unintentionally reinforced by cat lovers who give their young felines the green light to continue by petting them. In Smokey's mind, if you liked it when he did it as a kitten, why are you suddenly not such a big fan of feline grooming now that he has reached a hefty adult weight?

To stop his ear-fetish antics, stand up and walk out of the room as soon as he climbs up on you, wraps his paws around your neck, and makes the move to lick your lobes. Don't yell at him or toss him roughly away; just put him on the floor and leave. By walking away, you are taking away attention, something Smokey obviously seeks from you.

Now comes part two of the plan. Wait a few minutes and then return. Perform an activity that you both enjoy, like chasing a feather wand, teaching him a trick, or fetching a paper wad. Important: don't just walk away, but give Smokey an appropriate alternative to interact with you. After all, you don't want to weaken that wonderful bond between the two of you. If Smokey persists, you need a last-resort tactic. Make a noise he doesn't like such as clapping your hands loudly or making a hissing sound. The idea is to disrupt Smokey's behavior but not harm or frighten him.

## Wool-Sucking Fetish

**Q** My Siamese cat, Sake, is very dog-like in many ways. He fetches toys, he walks on a leash, and he comes when called. As wonderful as he is, he has one habit I would love to break. He chews and sucks on items made of wool. I find my wool socks saturated with slobber. It's disgusting. Why is he so obsessed with wool?

**A** Sake sounds a lot like my first cat, Corky, who was also a Siamese. When I was in junior high, my grandmother gave me a beautiful, charcoal gray sweater vest. I loved it and wore it a lot. That is, until the day I came home and found Corky on my bed sucking on my vest. I picked it up and there was a giant hole in the middle. I yelled at Corky and he fled from the room.

Little did I know then that wool sucking is not unusual among certain breeds, especially Siamese and Siamese crosses. In fact, veterinary researchers have discovered a strong genetic predisposition for this odd fetish. Experts report that Siamese cats represent about 50 percent of the wool-sucking feline population, though the reasons for this remain unclear. Most cats stop this behavior by the time they are two years old.

As for the behavior itself, it is not well understood. In addition to the genetic predisposition of some cats, one theory suggests that kittens removed from their mothers before six weeks of age are attracted to wool materials because they were not completely weaned. They seek out wool blankets and other clothing as a way to compensate for their shortened nursing time.

In the case of a confirmed wool addict, prevention is the best cure. You need to make a conscious effort to keep all wool clothing out of Sake's sight and away from his mouth. Stash your socks and sweaters in drawers and put other wool clothing in closets with doors completely closed. During the winter months, make sure that Sake cannot reach any wool blankets on your bed.

Next, make the object of his desire less desirable, such as spraying perfume on your wool clothing. As tempting as it may be, do not punish Sake — a mistake I made as a teenager with Corky. Yelling at him will only cause him to be more anxious and to be sneakier in his pursuit of the "forbidden" material.

Ask your veterinarian about Sake's diet. Some wool-sucking felines fare better when they are fed a high-fiber dry food. Finally, give Sake some "brain teasers," such as having him hunt for his food by putting kibble in treat balls or scattering it throughout a room. Provide him with plenty of interactive toys in several different rooms. The goal is to increase his activity level and prolong his feeding time to distract him from other pursuits.

# Cat Prefers Plastic Cuisine

**Q** I feed my 10-month-old kitten, Sunrise, twice a day, but lately I have caught him chewing on the electrical cords in my living room. I discovered his habit when I went to turn on a lamp. I thought the bulb had burned out until I noticed that the cord had been chewed in two. I've heard of cats eating weird things like tissue and newspaper, but what's the attraction to plastic cords? What can I do to stop him? I don't want him to accidentally electrocute himself or cause a fire.

**A** While many animals will eat non-food items (a habit called pica) because they develop dietary deficiencies, Sunshine is most likely chomping cords because he is bored. He needs more attention and stimulating activities to fill his day. Make sure he has toys to play with, a perch next to a window to look out of, and plenty of interaction with you.

Consider growing a pot or two of fresh grass for Sunrise to munch on indoors to satisfy his urge to nibble.

You're right to be concerned about the risk of sparking a fire in your house or having harm come to Sunrise. Fortunately, there are some effective products designed to cat-proof electrical cords. They are also easy to install. These cord covers are available through pet supply stores and catalogs. You can also apply an aversive spray formulated for pets to these cord covers to make them taste nasty.

# Making a Splash

**Q** I swear my cat is part raccoon! Chloe insists on putting her paws in her water bowl. Sometimes, she splashes around without taking a drink. She also makes a mess at mealtime by pawing out some of her food from the bowl and scattering it on the kitchen floor. She doesn't always eat these spilled pieces of food, and I'm forever cleaning up her messes. Can I change her behavior?

**A** In spite of their reputation for tolerating only dry land, many cats are actually water lovers. Some, such as Chloe, like to play in standing water, whereas others are fascinated by running water and prefer to drink from a faucet. There are a lot of theories as well as urban legends about this behavior, but no one knows for sure. This attraction to running water may reflect an adaptive behavior from a wild past. Perhaps because running water has fewer contaminants, many wild animals prefer to drink from streams than ponds.

Chloe's paw splashing could also be attributed to her need to test the water to make sure it is safe. The paw pad represents one of the most sensitive areas on a cat's body. Chloe is scooping water with her paw to check for possible "dangers" in the water or to test the temperature. Cats' long distance eyesight is superb and they see anything moving easily, but their close-up vision is somewhat weak.

They rely on their noses to sample food and paws to test water. And she may be partaking in a little fun and enjoying seeing the mini-ripples her paw creates in the bowl.

Please make sure that you provide Chloe with fresh water every day, even if she makes a mess. Offer her more than one bowl in your home. If you don't mind her perching on a bathroom sink, leave one with a few inches of water for her to play in during the day. You might consider an inexpensive automatic water dispenser that trickles water continuously. Many cats find these irresistible. These are readily available at pet supply stores and through catalogs.

Another idea is to take a one-gallon plastic jug and cut a hole about two inches from the bottom. Make the hole just a bit bigger than Chloe's head (don't forget to allow for her whiskers!) so that she can reach in for a drink but can't splash too much water on the floor. If she pushes the jug around, you can attach it to a wall.

As for Chloe's messy eating habit, first rule out any possible dental problems. Some cats with bad teeth or inflamed gums have difficulty chewing and swallowing kibble. Make sure Chloe's teeth and gums are healthy. If she checks out okay, then let me offer some suggestions.

Your cat might be bored with the same old chow every day. You can warm up dry food to bring out a more beckoning aroma, or you can make chowtime a bit of an adventure. Like you, I had a cat who seemed to take great delight in flinging her food around. I placed kibble in small piles in the kitchen and dining room for Sam to stalk, find, and consume. She had fun conquering her kibble and seemed quite satisfied with the arrangement. Try this with Chloe and praise her as she finds and eats her "prey." She may be more apt to get into the "hunt" of the food and less apt to toss the food around. A treat ball with holes might solve the problem too.

To contain the mess, forget placemats. They are simply too small. Opt instead for a large plastic drain board with a rim to prevent food from spreading across the floor. Or supersize your protective area with a plastic tablecloth that you can place on the kitchen floor during mealtime. The tablecloth can be easily taken outside to shake out excess crumbs and cleaned with a sponge. Then just fold it and tuck it in the pantry or closet until the next meal.

Finally, pay attention to what you serve the meals in. Some cats have definite preferences. Some like ceramic or steel better than plastic, which can impart an off odor or taste. Some like bowls with wide enough openings so that their whiskers don't touch the sides when they eat. Try serving Chloe's food in a wide-mouthed ceramic bowl if you are now using a plastic one. It may turn her into a neater eater.

> **FELINE DRINK TIP**
> Automatic drinking fountains for pets usually feature a charcoal filter to keep the water fresh and to absorb odors. The sound of the moving, circulating water attracts some cats. However you serve it up, water is necessary for your cat's overall health. Make sure there is always plenty of clean water available.

# Drooling with Delight

**Q** I call my home "the house of drool." Not only do I have Jimbo the bulldog, but I also have a cat who starts to drool when I pet him a lot. Bogart is a tabby I adopted a year ago from a local animal shelter, where he showed up as a stray looking for food. We think he is about three years old. He drools so much that I have to keep a washcloth within reach so I can wipe his mouth when he sits on my lap and purrs. Why does he drool?

**A** We know cats purr when they are content, but some felines also drool when they become relaxed and happy. Why they drool remains one of those feline mysteries in life. Just like Pavlov's famous dogs who drooled when they heard the dinner bell, Bogart has become conditioned to drool when he receives a certain type of affection. In your case, that is when he is on your lap and enjoying wonderful, loving petting from you. Count yourself fortunate that Bogart views you as a trusted ally, someone who lets him be his complete contented self — dripping drool and all.

Being stimulated on certain areas of the body may trigger his salivary response. Most likely, he drools when you massage his head, chin, and neck areas. Experiment by just petting those areas the next time he jumps on your lap. See if he starts to drool and for how long. Next time, restrict your petting to his back. Talk sweet to him. You may discover that he drools less when a less sensitive area is petted. You are smart to keep the washcloth handy to wipe his chin to keep the drool from dripping on your lap or your recliner — this is a hard behavior to correct. In some instances, however, drooling is due to a medical condition, so mention it to your veterinarian.

## Counter Commandos

**Q** When I come home in the evening, I always have to shoo Salt and Pepper, my pair of Persians, off my kitchen counters. I hate the thought of their litter-coated paws walking on counters where I do my food preparation. It's embarrassing when guests witness my cats jumping on the counters. They are great cats in so many other ways, but how can I break them of this disgusting habit?

**A** Salt and Pepper do belong in the kitchen, but in your spice rack and not on the counters. Feline counter surfing is an annoyance for many cat owners. I agree that it is unappetizing to think of dirty paws trespassing on eating surfaces. In addition, it can be quite dangerous. A curious cat can leap up on a hot stove or land on a sharp knife on a cutting board.

To keep your nimble felines off these places, you need to understand why they jump up there in the first place. Put yourself in your cat's mindset. The counter is high. Cats love to survey the scene from a safe and elevated perch. And kitchen counters offer an added bonus: they smell good. Even after a good scrubbing, counters still smell like broiled chicken, tuna casserole, or grilled steaks to cruising cats who hope to find some bits of leftover food not captured by your clean-up sponge.

Counter surfing can be rechanneled to safer

vertical places in your home. To do this, you must first make the dining room table and kitchen counters far less appealing. This requires that you "redecorate" these places temporarily to make them less attractive to your feline duo.

Start by placing double-sided tape on the edge of your counters and dining room table. Cats detest the feel of sticky tape on their paws. A good way to do this without having to pull up the tape when you want to cook or eat is to put double-sided tape on placemats and position them all over your counters.

In the middle of the counter, position a couple of cookie sheets (the kind with sides) filled with water. A cat who bypasses the sticky tape will land with a splash and scoot off. The tape and shallow pans cannot be seen from floor level, which adds a surprise element. A third tactic is to use cleaners on your counters that contain citrus, an aroma cats hate.

You can also go high tech, but bring out your checkbook. There are several motion detectors on the market designed to dissuade cats from leaping on counters. When the cat jumps on a counter, an alarm sounds and quick spurts of harmless air are released. That would be enough to startle me from trying to trespass where I didn't belong!

It is equally important to offer a suitable place or two for your cats to dwell from on high. If they find a spot in a bookcase or even a mantelpiece that is acceptable to you, keep it clear for them. I recommend placing a sturdy cat tree or climbing tree in a high-traffic area of your house, such as the corner of the living room, where the cats can check out all the household activities from a lofty perch. Or place one of these trees next to a window for

**FELINE FACT**

A cat can jump about seven times as high as he is tall.

your cats to check out what's happening in your neighborhood. Entice your cats to use these trees by sprinkling some catnip and leave treats for them to discover when you are gone. Reward them with special treats when you find them on these trees.

# Favorite Feline Tunes

**Q** My cat is extremely fearful and seems to panic at the least change in routine. I've read that certain music can help calm cats. Is that true? If so, what type of music works best?

**A** If you're searching for a way to calm your feline, the answer may be harp therapy. It is well documented that music therapy can provide a welcome distraction or pleasure for people, especially those hospitalized with cancer or coping with terminal diseases. Music can minimize pain, decrease anxiety, and serve as a powerful distraction for patients. The same seems to hold true for our pets.

Sue Raimond, a concert violinist and composer, is considered the pioneer of harp enrichment and therapy for pets. An expert in the field of cytocymatics and vibroacoustics, she serves as an adjunct lecturer specializing in pain management at the University of California at San Diego. She has tested the effects of harp music on wolves, dogs, cats, goats, sheep, donkeys, and gorillas and authored several studies on her research.

Her harp therapy is drawing the interest of leading veterinarians and animal behaviorists who see music as a complementary tool in modifying undesirable behavior that might be caused by stress in family pets. Veterinary schools such as Cummings School of Veterinary Medicine at Tufts University and UC-Davis in California, recommend her CDs for pets with separation anxiety.

Dr. Patrick Melese, a veterinarian and certified applied animal behaviorist in San Diego, recommends playing harp music for overly anxious pets, saying that the music does indeed help some anxious cats and dogs to calm down, relax, and eventually go to sleep. Other experts agree and add that classical music seems to tame the beast inside your tabby. Possible benefits include lower heart rates and blood pressure levels, slower breathing, elevated endorphin levels, and decreased stress hormones. It is thought that listening to music decreases stress and anxiety in animals awaiting surgery and helps speed recovery time.

So, how does harp therapy work? Raimond says that a plucked string sends overtones — some inaudible to the human ear — like a dog whistle. The sound produces harmonic overtones that seem to work at a cellular level in lowering blood pressure and reducing stress levels, though scientific research is needed to validate this. If you think this all sounds a bit New Age-y, you're not far off-key. But this work is worth considering as researchers study the healing power of music in human health.

Whenever Raimond needs to transport her cats to the veterinary clinic, she pops a CD containing the harp music into her car's stereo as she makes the 20-minute drive. She says that all three cats yowl if the music is not on but remain calm when she plays the music. She says for the music to work, a cat must hear it for at least three minutes. Generally at that point, Raimond says most cats will start to settle down. Within 10 to 20 minutes, most cats lie down in a resting state with some even sleeping soundly. Now that sounds like sweet music to everyone's ears.

# Bathing Beauty

**Q** Whenever I take a bubble bath, my cat scoots into the bathroom as soon as she hears the water flowing. She perches on the side of the tub while I bathe. Once she slipped and fell in! Even getting covered in bubbles didn't deter her and she was back the next night. What's the big deal about bathtime?

**A** As explained in Making a Splash on page 126, many cats are fascinated by running water, whether the source is a bathtub, sink, or shower faucet. Some cats will even sit on the edge of the tub while the shower is running. But a bubble bath has a special allure. Think about it — when you are in the tub, you are usually relaxed, quiet, and not moving much, traits that appeal to the average feline. And the bubbles provide a fascinating texture at which to bat.

I say enjoy these quiet moments with your cat. There is no harm in her hanging out with you, and your feline friend won't gossip to others as to what you look like in your "birthday suit." I encourage you to call for your cat before you turn on the faucet. This way, you can reinforce the *come* command in a welcoming setting. Then let those bubbles flow and enjoy your kitty's company as you soak.

---

# Santa's Unwelcome Helper

**Q** Every year when we put up our Christmas tree, our cat, Leo, decides to test his climbing skills. I find ornaments — some broken — on the living room floor each morning. Once he actually leaped on the tree with such force that he knocked it over. What can I do to stop Leo from bothering our tree during the holidays?

**A** Christmas often brings out the imp in cats, whose favorite carol must be "wreck the halls with paws of folly." Many cats are curious about new objects that appear in their territory, especially ones as interesting as a real tree. Leo probably loves that fresh pine scent as much as you do. He thinks of it as a wonderful early holiday gift — the smell of the great outdoors.

Another major temptation is all those glimmering ornaments and shimmering tinsel. Many cats like shiny objects. Leo has discovered that a slight bat of the paw makes these objects move and another bat turns them into fun toys that skitter across the floor.

A third attraction can be what's under the tree. If catnip toys and gifts of food are wrapped and placed under the tree a few days before Santa's scheduled arrival, Leo doesn't know to wait until December 25. Wait to put those gifts under the tree until you're ready to open presents with your family.

Following on the next page are some other ways to make your tree less attractive, or at least safer, for Leo.

◆ Put a hook in your ceiling or at the top of the window nearest the tree and use high-strength fishing line to anchor the tree in place. Two hooks are even better!

◆ Position your most-prized ornaments and any breakable ones on the upper branches or consider displaying them somewhere other than the tree, like on a mantelpiece or bookcase. Use nonbreakable ornaments whenever possible on the tree.

◆ Place nonbreakable cat toys on the floor near the tree to distract your curious kitty.

◆ Put orange or grapefruit peels under the tree. Cats dislike the scent of citrus.

◆ Consider keeping Leo in a different room that features plenty of feline amenities to prevent any holiday mischief when you are out of the house or asleep.

◆ Cats love to play with and chew on shiny, rustling tinsel and glitter, but they can become quite ill if they swallow it. Either forego it altogether or hang it only on the highest branches.

◆ Cover your tree stand with a tree skirt or a colorful tablecloth so that your cat can't sip from the water reservoir. The water could make him sick.

# A Feline Curtain Call

**Q** We live in an old house we inherited from my grandmother. We love our antique furniture and the wonderful curtains adorning the big picture window in our living room. But my cat, Reggie, insists on climbing the curtains. When I yell at him to get off, he does, but I can't watch him all the time. Unfortunately, the curtains are showing some claw marks. What can we do to save our curtains?

**A** Cats are born climbers with a need to be in high places. Your beloved antique curtains are a feline version of those rock-climbing walls that attract weekend athletes.

Here are some options for consideration. You can booby-trap the curtains by balancing a few aluminum soda cans on the curtain rods. Tape a few coins into each one to increase the shock value. The sound of these cans crashing to the floor should startle your curtain climber and convince him that they are too scary for further adventures.

Or, you can temporarily hang a curtain or light blanket on the rods. When Reggie tries to scale the curtains, he won't be able to grip and climb. The curtain or blanket will fall to the ground, discouraging your explorer. Or try temporarily folding the curtains in half over the rods. You can also spray a citrus scent or other aversive odor at the bottom third of the curtains as a deterrent.

These temporary tactics are designed to communicate to Reggie the curtains are anything but appealing or safe. Once this happens, you can restore your desired decorative look.

Clearly, Reggie needs a suitable outlet to show off his climbing talents. In addition to discouraging him from climbing the curtains, provide him with a carpeted cat tree. If you have floor to ceiling posts, consider wrapping one in sisal rope. Then applaud as Reggie performs amazing feline gymnastic maneuvers. If you have the room, you might lean a large branch or log in one corner for him to clamber on. You could also hang a rope hammock with one end attached high on a wall and the other end to the floor. If it's the view that is attracting him, try a window platform for him to perch on.

As a last resort, you may wish to replace those curtains with window blinds. In cat households, vertical blinds are a better choice than horizontal ones. They are far more difficult to climb, even for the most agile of felines.

# Holy Tissue Terror

**Q** It's a good thing that toilet paper and tissues are inexpensive. Our Abyssinian cat, Abigail, seems to get a big kick out of rolling all the paper off the toilet roll and stealing tissues from the box and shredding them into tiny pieces. We try to remember to close the bathroom door when we leave, but Abigail seizes any opportunities to destroy our paper products. Any explanations and suggestions?

**A** Abyssinians embody the word active. They hate being bored and will make their own fun if they need to. Clearly, Abigail needs more playtime and more stimulating games to focus her attention and energy on. Let me offer you a few remedies to help when you forget to close the bathroom door:

◆ Turn the tissue boxes upside down when not in use, making it much harder for Abigail to snatch a tissue and start shredding.

◆ Install a toilet roll dispenser that covers the top of the toilet roll and prevents paws from grabbing the end of the sheet and unraveling the roll.

◆ Cover a tissue with an aversive spray and place it on top of the tissue box or toilet paper roll to discourage your playful friend.

◆ Booby-trap the roll by perching a small cup of water on it. Try a half-cup measuring cup. Getting doused by water will discourage even the most determined paper-shredding cat.

# Why Filbert Turned Wacky

**THE OWNER OF A 16-WEEK-OLD KITTEN** came into my clinic feeling totally dumbfounded. Her once sweet, playful kitten was either staring off into space like a zombie, or hissing and growling like he was possessed by the devil. It was clear from the start of my physical exam that something was amiss. For one thing, the black-and-white kitten was significantly underweight.

"He hasn't grown very much since we got him, even though he seems to eat pretty well," said the owner. Filbert was mentally dull in the exam room, showing no interest in chasing or following a bell on a string. For a normal kitten, this is unheard of.

A complete blood count, serum chemistry panel, and urinalysis were submitted. Filbert's blood count showed microcytosis — smaller than normal red blood cells. The chemistry panel revealed elevations in several liver enzymes. These findings were highly suggestive of a congenital liver disorder. One more blood test, called a bile acid test, was necessary to confirm my suspicions. As I suspected, the bile acid test showed that the kitten had a portosystemic shunt (PSS).

A PSS is an anatomical defect in which most of the blood from the intestinal tract bypasses or is shunted around the liver. The liver is unable to detoxify the blood properly, and the toxins go into the general circulation where they cause a variety of clinical signs. Some signs

are physical, such as drool-
ing, tremors, stunted
growth, dilated pupils,
vomiting, diarrhea,
excessive thirst, and
urination. Often cats
will show behavioral
signs as well, such as
lethargy, stupor, staring off into space, or aggression. We
call this hepatic encephalopathy, which roughly translates
as a mental disorder resulting from a liver disorder.

An abdominal ultrasound revealed an "extrahepatic"
shunt, that is, a single blood vessel responsible for diverting
the blood from the intestinal tract around the liver, necessi-
tating a complicated surgery.

After his discharge, Filbert's owners reported that his
original spunky, affectionate personality quickly returned.
Six weeks later, Filbert was brought to me for neutering,
and I witnessed the transformation myself. His curiosity
and fidgeting made it impossible to listen to his heart.
When I finally could restrain him long enough to put the
stethoscope on his chest, it was still impossible to hear
his heart because he was purring too loudly!

Filbert's case is a classic example of how a behavioral
condition (hepatic encephalopathy) can be the result of
an anatomical disorder (portosystemic shunt).

*Contributed by Arnold Plotnick, DVM*

# Dead Bird on My Bed!

**Q** My cat, Lucy, uses the doggy door to go into our fenced backyard. We have a bird feeder out there, and every once in a while, I discover a dead bird on my pillow. I almost faint at the sight. I want to scold Lucy, but she looks at me with such pride. Lucy is about eight years old, but she is as healthy as a kitten. Why is she doing this?

**A** Cats have novel ways of showing that they love us and that they are worthy hunters. My Callie once presented me with a huge dead rat — like you, I nearly fainted. Whether these "gifts" are dead birds, rats, or crickets, our cats are displaying their hunting instincts. We may keep their food bowls full, but our domesticated cats are not hunting out of hunger.

Some cats do bring their prey back home with plans to snack later, but most just leave the carcass lying around. Experts in feline behavior speculate that cats may bring us these "gifts" in an effort to train us. Perhaps they have realized what lousy hunters we are. Or maybe they do it because they want our approval. They can't go out and buy expensive gifts on charge cards, so they hunt and offer us what they view as valued presents.

In any case, you can't snuff out Lucy's need to hunt. It's hardwired in her brain. (See Predator or Prey, page 12.) Instead, give those prey critters more of a fighting chance by putting a bell on Lucy's collar. If your cat goes outdoors, you probably shouldn't put up bird feeders — keep those for indoor cats to enjoy watching from the window. As an alternative, offer Lucy some fake prey to stalk and chase in your home, such as battery-operated toy mice that move erratically. Happy hunting!

# My Cat Acts Like a Pig

**Q** I always thought cats were fastidious and well groomed, but my cat is a dirt magnet. She loves to roll in the dirt outside. She digs in my herb garden and happily sports dirty paws and belly. Her beautiful black coat becomes all messy and dusty. Why does she do this?

**A** In general cats do pride themselves on sporting well-coiffed coats, and they spend hours each day grooming. However, your cat is on a mission motivated by scent and texture. Although it is common for dogs to roll in smelly things like dead fish and duck droppings, most cats don't seek out stinky spots, choosing instead to wriggle in dirt or on pavement. They do this for many reasons.

The main one is to loosen and remove dead hair to assist in their daily grooming sessions. The dirt and dust that sift down to the skin discourage fleas and other pests. Cats may also roll in dirt and garden soil to get rid of unwanted smells such as your Aunt Kate's potent perfume or Cousin Jim's smelly cigar. Plus a good roll on a scratchy surface just feels good, like a mini-massage!

My cat Callie used to roll whenever I took her outside, but now I help her stay clean by brushing her regularly so that her mostly white coat doesn't get dusty. She enjoys the attention and the brush feels just as good as rolling on my brick walkway.

Many cats will roll over on the ground when they see a friendly human approaching. It seems to be a way of saying, "I trust you enough to show you my belly; maybe you'll come over and scratch my ears since I'm so cute!" Of course, often when you approach, your cat will leap up and dash away, so who knows what she is really thinking?

You mention your herb garden. Your cat's nose is leading her to this scent-sensational spot where she can enjoy the feel of the dirt on the pads of her feet and the welcoming aroma of your garden goodies. Rolling in the dirt just adds to the pleasure of being outdoors.

# Crazy for Catnip

**Q** I hope you can settle a family bet. I say that all cats react to the smell of catnip, but my husband insists that they don't. Our cat, Gigi, comes running when I sprinkle fresh catnip on her cat tree. She races up the tree and starts rolling in the catnip and eating it. She loves it. But my husband had a cat who totally ignored catnip. When it comes to catnip, what's the deal with cats?

**A** I hope you didn't bet money with your husband, because he wins this friendly bet. Cats of all sizes, from domesticated tabbies to mountain lions, have been known to roll over, rub their faces, and twist their bodies in patches of this aromatic herb. Researchers report that up to 70 percent of cats exposed to catnip display some type of reaction and that the level of response appears to be influenced by genetics. Kittens don't appreciate catnip until they are at least six weeks old and about 30 percent of adult cats show no reaction at all. Different cats, even from the same litter, can display different responses to catnip, ranging from no reaction to total bliss to irritability.

Catnip *(Nepeta cataria)* is a member of the mint family. The oil from catnip leaves contains a chemical called nepetalactone, the odor of which closely resembles a substance present in a female cat's urine. Researchers do not know how the stimulus works, but the nepetalactone must be inhaled to reach the vomeronasal smell receptors and trigger a reaction. Most cats will rub their chins and cheeks or roll their entire bodies in catnip, while some cats also lick and chew it. The effects last, on average, from five to fifteen minutes.

A pinch or two of fresh or dried catnip is enough to bring out the wild antics in your cat. It is interesting to note that this psychosexual response cannot be triggered again for at least another hour after being exposed to catnip. For some reason, cats need some time between servings of catnip to reset their senses. Offer your cats some catnip about 20 minutes before bedtime. The herb should stimulate them to do enough exercise to become tired enough to sleep through the night.

I recommend that you treat your cat to toys filled with organic catnip, the highest quality of this feline-favorite herb. Store loose catnip in an airtight, dry container out of direct sunlight. Do not keep catnip in the refrigerator because the cold and damp will weaken the herb's potency.

You might try making a cup of fresh steeped catnip tea for yourself. For humans, catnip works as a sedative, not a stimulant, making it a perfect choice to help us fall into dreamland.

## HONEYSUCKLE, ANYONE?

If your cat is not a fan of catnip, then try giving him toys filled with honeysuckle sawdust or a chunk of honeysuckle wood. You can find them in pet supply stores and online. The *Lonicera tartarica* species of the honeysuckle shrub elicits a similar though less intense reaction than catnip. You must moisten the honeysuckle to activate its odor.

Do not let your cat chew on raw honeysuckle wood or berries, however, and be aware that some varieties of honeysuckle are toxic.

Here's an interesting tidbit to share with your feline-loving friends: Scientists report that about 30 percent of all cats (the ones who show no reaction to catnip) respond to the honeysuckle aroma.

# Game of Cat and Computer Mouse

**Q** I work from home and love having my cat, Spam, in the home office with me. He usually sleeps on a cat bed on the corner of my desk. I spend a lot of time at the computer and sometimes Spam insists on walking on my keyboard or standing between me and the computer monitor. It's annoying to have to keep moving him. I also worry that he might step on the wrong key and I will lose data on my computer. I don't want to shut him out of the office. Any suggestions?

**A** Computers and cats don't mix. A cat walking and sitting on the keyboard, perching on the monitor, and rubbing against computer towers can shut down applications, delete files, type gibberish into word documents, or cause hard drives to crash. I too enjoy having my cats nearby while I work at the computer. One of my cats frequently positioned herself between my computer monitor and me until I realized that she was broadcasting a need for my attention. So, I put a cat bed on a spare office chair and rolled it next to my chair. Contented, she no longer tries to tap dance on my keyboard while I'm tapping on the keys.

Keeping cats off keyboards is trickier than keeping them off counters. Spam already has his own spot of real estate on your desk, so your job is to teach him that he is not allowed in your work area. You cannot risk squirting him with water because you don't want to damage your expensive equipment. When he climbs on your keyboard, pick him up and put him on the floor. You might have to do this repeatedly at first, but he should eventually figure out that the computer is off-limits.

Play a different game of cat and mouse by tossing a toy mouse across the room as a diversion from your keyboard. You can also engage your cat in some fun play for 10 to 15 minutes before you start work on the computer so he will be more likely to catnap. Also, make sure he has eaten before you settle down to your tasks, so he isn't pestering you for a snack. Sometimes just picking up your cat and cuddling him for a few minutes will satisfy his need for attention and he will wander off to find other amusement.

If you have a cat who plays with your keyboard when you're not around, install a retracting shelf that you can push under your desk when not in use so it's not accessible to your curious cat. Or just use a hard plastic keyboard cover when you're not typing.

You can also fight back with a high-tech tool: Paw-Sense, a software program that protects computers by foiling felines. The program detects the weight of a cat on a keyboard and blocks the random action from entering commands to your programs or operating system. A message appears on the monitor screen that reads "Cat-like typing detected." To unblock the computer, you type the word "Human." Purchasers have the option of selecting an annoying sound that is activated when a paw steps on the keyboard, even if you are not in the room.

The simplest solution: keep your home office door shut when you are working on the computer. Make it a no-cats-allowed zone. I know you don't want this option, but you might try it for a day or two and see if that is enough to discourage your keyboard-loving cat.

---

# Funny-face Feline

**Q** What is happening with my cat, Mambo? On occasion, he seems to get into a hypnotic state when he sniffs something very intently. He opens his mouth slightly, wrinkles his nose, grimaces, and curls back his lips. It is such a strange-looking pose. It usually happens when he smells some bushes. I've never seen him do it in the house. Is this something only cats do? What does it mean?

**A** Mambo is exhibiting the Flehmen response. That funny face he makes is not limited to cats. Many other mammals, including lions, bats, and horses, strike this pose in response to particular smells. Mambo's nose is alerting him to possible female cats in heat or male trespassers in the neighborhood. The interesting scent in this case is urine.

The scientific explanation is that as Mambo draws in air, he sends the odor through a specialized sac known as Jacobson's organ or the vomeronasal organ. This organ is located in the roof of the mouth, where it traps odor molecules and dispatches information to the brain. Flehmen can occur with many scents, but it generally happens when an animal — male or female — smells urine.

Mambo is pinning down pheromones, chemical substances generated by animals that serve as a form of aromatic communication. One deep sniff and Mambo can access all sorts of information about another animal as if that critter left a business card. He can assess the gender, reproductive status, and health of other animals who left marks along your walk. If you want to get the real lowdown on neighborhood gossip, ask Mambo — his nose truly knows!

---

# Lap of Luxury

**Q** All of the cats I've had before Jessie were content with sitting next to me or near me. Not Jessie.

She insists on climbing into my lap and settling down and purring. She is very quick. Often when I sit down, she comes out of nowhere a few seconds later and leaps into my lap. She can sit anywhere. Why does she want to be in my lap all of the time?

**A** Cats are like people. They have distinct preferences for where they feel most comfortable. My cat Little Guy is very sweet, but I long ago stopped trying to make him into a lap cat. He is uncomfortable there, so I respect his desire to plop next to me on the sofa.

For felines who love to cuddle, laps offer three benefits. First, laps are elevated. Cats like to roost up off the floor where they can survey the activities around them. Second, laps are warm. Our body heat attracts cats, especially during the colder months. Third, laps are safe. Snuggling with a favorite person, a cat enjoys a sense of security.

Some cats take advantage of their one-on-one moments with you to dig their claws in a rhythmic motion up and down (ouch!) on your legs. (See The Need to Knead, page 30.) Kneading helps them relive those glory kitten days when they nursed on their mothers and felt totally safe and secure. You might enjoy this bonding time more if you trim your cat's nails or place a folded blanket or towel across your lap to protect your thighs.

Count yourself fortunate you have a lovable lap-seeking feline friend in Jessie. Her presence in your lap can serve to bring you feelings of contentment and relaxation as well.

# The Cat-Crinkle Connection

**Q** My cat can be snoozing, but if I take a piece of paper or cellophane or foil and form it into a wad, she instantly wakes up and looks like she is ready for a hunt. She loves crinkly sounds and will run after a paper ball if I toss it down the hallway. If I rattle a paper grocery bag, she comes running. She will actually jump inside the bag if I leave it on the floor. What's the big attraction of crinkly-sounding objects for cats?

**A** Even though these everyday household items are inanimate, the crinkling sounds they produce mimic the high-pitched chatter of birds, crickets, mice, and rats, thereby triggering a cat's predatory response. Your cat's imagination is fully engaged as she pretends these items are the real deal. You are giving her the chance to hone her hunting skills and show off a bit in front of you.

Some cats show the same interest in shiny objects. A few breeds, specifically Manx, Japanese Bobtails, and Munchkins, have a tendency to collect and hoard glittery objects, such as jewelry and silver coins, and stash them in strange places, such as inside a shoe or underneath a recliner.

**FELINE FACT**

Munchkins, a breed of dwarf cats, possess short legs due to a dominant gene mutation. They are named after the little people in the movie classic *The Wizard of Oz*.

## MANX MANIA

The tailless Manx is one of the oldest cat breeds, but its history is a mystery. According to a biblically inspired Celtic folktale, the Manx cat was the last of God's creatures to climb aboard the ark, barely making it before Noah slammed the door shut, cutting off its tail. Upset, the cat fled the ark and swam from Ararat to the Isle of Man, where it found a home.

Another folktale claims that the Irish stole kittens to use their tails as good-luck charms. To save their kittens, wise mother cats bit off the tails of their young, thus producing the tailless cat.

The real reason behind the missing tails? It is likely that the breed developed from cats dropped on the Isle of Man, an island in the Irish Sea between England and Ireland, by visiting ships. Centuries of inbreeding in an isolated environment resulted in a spontaneous mutation and the disappearance of a tail from this friendly, affectionate breed.

Some Manx cats do have tails, either full or partial length, and although still considered pedigreed, they cannot be shown in championship classes at official shows. Only the completely tailless "rumpy" Manx and the "rumpy riser" Manx with one or two vertebrae can compete, though cats with "stumpy" tails or the rare "longies" with an almost normal length tail are still valuable for breeding or as pets.

# Sky-High Tail

**Q** My cat, JJ, instantly raises his butt and tail high in the air whenever I pet him or scratch his back. It's obvious that he enjoys the contact. He doesn't seem to mind that he is "mooning" me with his rear end, but I don't like it. Why does he do this and can I get him to stop?

**A** JJ is demonstrating what's known among feline fans as "elevator butt." You push the right button by scratching just the right spot, and he can't help but raise his butt up high. After all, he has been doing it since birth.

Kittens raise their back ends and hoist their tails high for their mothers to inspect and clean. This early stimulation was both functional and pleasurable. Now as an adult, JJ's so-called mooning is just his way of telling you that you are worthy of scratching a sensitive area that feels good to him.

Stopping JJ's hardwired behavior would be like trying to keep your eyes open when you sneeze. It's impossible. Just relax and appreciate his enjoyment of your attention. If he performs this in front of company (and you know he will), let humor be your guide and simply declare that it is "elevator butt" time. If it embarrasses you, don't scratch his back in front of your guests!

# Extra! Extra! Read All about It!

**Q** One of my morning rituals is sipping a cup of coffee while I read the daily newspaper on my sofa. Since I adopted Gizmo, a very playful Bobtail, I barely get a chance to scan the front-page headlines before he is leaping and landing on my paper. He has surprised me a few times and I've ended up spilling coffee everywhere. Why is he doing this?

**A** Cats can't read, of course, but they are intensely curious. Gizmo is a member of a lively, playful breed, so he is even more interested in what you are doing and in trying to capture your attention. When he opts to take a closer look, he leaps in — literally.

Try this solution: take a few sheets from sections you don't read, perhaps the classified ads. Prop them up like a tent on the floor next to you. Tap on the sides to attract Gizmo's attention. Hide a favorite toy or a small treat under the pages. Encourage him to leap and pounce and dive on his own part of the paper, leaving the front page, the sports section, and the comics for your eyes only.

You can also turn unwanted sections of the newspaper into a magical carpet ride for your cat. Place them at the start of a long uncarpeted hallway and encourage your cat to take a running start, leap on the paper, and slide down the hall. I've discovered that the slick ad supplements work far better than the actual news sections of your paper.

## STRAYS TURNED STARS

Shamu the killer whale may be the main headliner at Sea World, but dozens of talented cats are making a splash of their own at the theme park. The former strays star in a zany show called "Pets Rule," which also features dogs, birds, and a confident pot-bellied pig. Felines who jump from a 10-foot tower onto the shoulders of a trainer prove that cats can perform with the same skill as dogs and whales.

During the show, cats and dogs rush onto the stage from various entry points — all off leash and all undistracted by the applauding audience. The cats traverse tightropes, run through tunnels, and weave between the legs of a striding trainer. In one scene, three black cats leap into a gigantic milk bottle on stage and three white cats leap out.

Renowned animal trainer Joel Slaven told me there is nothing more gratifying than adopting a shy, untrained cat from a shelter and seeing it transform into a confident and happy performer. Slaven purposely selects cats who were surrendered because of unwanted behaviors such as curtain climbing, countertop prowling, and top-shelf leaping.

Slaven has found that the most trainable cats are those with good attention spans and outgoing personalities and who are highly motivated by food, praise, or grooming sessions. He observes each cat's natural behaviors and selects tricks based on preferred activities. A cat who likes to climb drapes, for instance, can be trained to climb a rope. A cat who trips you by rubbing against your legs could be directed into weaving in and out of legs on cue.

Slaven identifies patience and a positive attitude as two keys to feline training success. He builds on each small accomplishment and conducts brief training sessions, encouraging the cats with praise and treats.

## MANY, MANY TOES

Count the number of toes on your cat's front paw — it should total five. Now check the back paw — you should count four toes. Some cats, however, sport as many as seven toes on each paw. Having extra toes, or being polydactyl, is a congenital abnormality but not a health concern. Any feline breed can sport extra toes, though the CFA does not register polydactyl cats for showing.

Legend has it that seventeenth-century sailors regarded polydactyl cats as lucky, because the added toes made them better hunters and gave them better balance during rocky weather.

Visitors to the home of the late great writer (and cat lover) Ernest Hemingway come not only to marvel at his way with words but to meet and greet the numerous polydactyl cats roaming the grounds. About 60 live on his estate and are protected by the terms of his will. That explains why polydactyl cats are sometimes nicknamed "Hemingway cats." Other admirers call them "thumb cats" or "mitten cats."

# PART IV

# Thinking Outside the Box

As editor of *Catnip,* I receive questions every week from readers puzzled or panicked by their cats' bathroom behavior. This is serious stuff for people and literally life-or-death for far too many cats. The number one behavioral reason cats are booted out of homes and discarded at animal shelters is because of inappropriate elimination.

Owners understandably become tired of cleaning up messes on their carpets, floors, and even their beds. Or one spouse will deliver an ultimatum: either persuade the cat to use the litter box or get rid of the cat.

There are many reasons why some cats bypass the litter box and go elsewhere. The true cause may be a medical condition or stress-induced changes in the home routine or a dislike of the available "facilities." Either way, your cat is conveying that something is wrong. It is up to you to act like a pet detective and track down clues.

In this section, I share some scenarios with the hope that my answers enable you and your cat to enjoy many happy and incident-free years together in a home that always smells like a beautiful spring day.

# Litter Box Lessons

**Q** We're planning to adopt our first kitten soon. I thought kittens knew instinctively how to use a litter box from day one, but my friends with young cats say that isn't always the case. If the kitten we bring home needs help learning how to use the litter box, what's the best way to train her?

**A** I bet you never imagined that someday you would add "litter box tutor" to your list of accomplishments. It may not be as impressive as brain surgeon or world's best mom, but for your young kitten, a little litter box guidance will go a long way in ensuring she practices a lifetime of good bathroom habits.

True, most kittens take to litter like, well, grown cats take to catnip. Cats instinctively bury their feces and cover

up urine deposits, a behavior that dates back thousands of years to when wild cats needed to avoid detection by possible predators. That's why outdoor cats choose the garden or sandbox for toileting, much to the dismay of gardeners and parents.

Most kittens learn the basic ABCs of litter box lessons from their mothers by about four weeks of age. It's a

## WHY CATS LOSE THEIR HOMES

The National Council on Pet Population Study and Policy offers a comprehensive look at why cats are relinquished to animal shelters. When looking strictly at behavioral reasons, house soiling was the top reason, coming in at 43.2 percent. Overall, this council reports the following top reasons for cats being surrendered to shelters:

- ◆ Human lifestyle (too many cats in home, allergies, personal problems)
- ◆ Housing issues (moving, landlord issues, inadequate facilities)
- ◆ Behavioral problems (house soiling, issues with other pets)

case of kittens see, kittens do, in their quest to mimic the actions of their wise moms. Kittens who are orphaned or weaned away from their mothers at a very early age may be clueless about litter box etiquette. Or they may just be slow learners.

Here are some tips to help your new kitten ace her litter lessons and get off on the right paw:

♦ Purchase a small litter box with low sides (no higher than three inches) so your short-legged kitten can easily climb in and out. Large litter boxes with sides four inches or higher or the kind with hoods can be too intimidating for some small kittens.

♦ Locate the litter box in a place in your house that is easy to access but not in a noisy, high-traffic area like the kitchen. Never place the litter box near the food and water bowls. Cats are clean creatures and abhor the notion of having their chow next to their bathroom. If you live in a multilevel house, locate a litter box on each level.

♦ When you bring home your new kitten, escort her to the litter box (filled with about two inches of litter) and place her in the box. Gently move her front paws through the litter to let her feel the texture. Use your index finger to paw through the clean litter. Then let her explore the litter box and jump out on her own.

- During the first few days of her arrival, place her in the litter box when she first wakes up, after she eats, after a play session, and after she wakes from a catnap.

- After placing her in the litter box, quietly step back and leave her be. Unlike puppies who love to hear their owner sing out "Good potty!" in a happy voice, most felines prefer privacy and don't wish for you to bring out the band or applaud when they accomplish their mission. Be more subdued with your kitten.

- Be sure to scoop out the deposits daily to keep the litter box clean.

Please practice the Two P's of Potty Training: Patience and Punishment-Free. It may take your youngster just a few trips to the litter box to get the hang of things or it may take a few weeks. Resist the temptation to scold or yell or squirt her with a water bottle, because the punishment approach usually backfires. Your kitten may become so frightened that she starts to avoid the litter box and hunts for less scary places like under your bed or in your closet.

If you notice any signs of diarrhea or if you see your kitten straining or hear her crying when using the litter box, please take her to your veterinarian to be examined for a possible medical problem such as a urinary tract infection or intestinal parasites. Good luck!

**SECRETS TO SUCCESS**

Develop the habit of scooping out the urine and feces from the litter box daily. Every two weeks, remove the litter entirely and clean the box with mild dishwashing soap and warm water. If possible, allow the box to air-dry in the sun to kill germs. If you do use bleach to disinfect the box, use a very weak solution and rinse thoroughly before drying. The strong odor of bleach can be a turnoff to your cat.

I recommend that you have a spare litter box to fill with fresh litter while the other box is drying. If you have multiple boxes, clean one at time so your cats can always find a spot to go.

# Litany of Litter

**Q** Help! I am confused by all the types of litter available at the store. Litter can be made of clay, crumbled corn, and even recycled newspapers. There are regular types, clumping types, and some that are flushable. Some litter is scented and some is not. And it can be pricey. What's the best kind to buy?

**A** You're right. Litter is not cheap, and it is not lightweight. Sharing a home with three cats tugs on my wallet and taxes my forearm muscles each time I lug home another big bag of the stuff.

Litter has evolved in the same commercial manner as coffee. Remember the days when your choices in coffee were either black or with cream and sugar? Now, instead of ordering a plain cup of Joe, we need to know words like mocha, latte, and espresso.

Litter first hit store shelves more than 50 years ago. Credit a clever young guy named Edward Lowe who worked in his dad's industrial absorbent company. One day, a friend complained to him about the smell and the mess of using dirt and ash in a box for her cat. Lowe suggested she sprinkle some of the company's absorbent material in the box to quell the hold-your-nose odor. Voilà! The birth of litter.

Today, a litany of litter is available. Most brands claim to control odors, but that is arguable. Clay ranks as the most popular choice because it forms clumps that are easy to scoop. However, clay dust can cause respiratory issues in people and cats.

Environmentally minded companies have created litter made of pine and grain that absorbs well and is biodegradable. Grain contains a natural enzyme that tones down the powerful ammonia odor in cat urine. A new generation of litter choices include recycled paper, flushable green tea leaves, silica, and silica gel. Some litters come with ingredients such as baking soda, perfumes, or citrus that are touted to oust odors.

To help you narrow your choices, keep in mind that a feline's nose is at least 100 times more sensitive than a person's nose. In addition, cats are not big fans of citrus or perfume smells. What your nose may detect as a light, welcoming hint of citrus can overpower a "scent-sitive" cat and might even evoke a litter box boycott. This also applies to deodorizing products that stick on walls or litter boxes. Nix that idea and use air-purifying machines next to the boxes instead.

Size also matters to most cats. Put yourself in your cat's paws for a moment. Would you rather walk on a fine-grained surface or a rocky road filled with large-size pellets? Your cat may be part of the feline majority and prefer the fine-grained clumping clay or could surprise you by liking the large pellet type.

In summary, put your cat's needs and desires first. Test her preferences by buying small bags of a couple different types of litter. Put one in one litter box and the other in a second box and see which one your cat visits repeatedly. One sure sign that your cat does not like the choice of litter is if he eliminates right next to the box. He is showing you that he is trying to do the right thing, but he doesn't want to come in contact with that type of litter.

# The Case of Tom

**WHEN PAT AND PETER BROUGHT TOM**, their eight-month-old neutered male cat to my office, they informed me that he was acting lethargic, was not interested in food, and had started eating his litter.

On physical exam, Tom's gums were white. A blood test revealed that Tom was dangerously anemic. Anemia can be categorized as "regenerative," meaning that the bone marrow is trying to replenish the bloodstream with new red blood cells, or "nonregenerative," meaning that the bone marrow is not replenishing red blood cells. I ordered several tests and, given the severity of his anemia, gave Tom a life-saving blood transfusion.

Over a few days, Tom's blood tests revealed that he had a nonregenerative anemia. To figure out why, I obtained a sample of bone marrow and the analysis revealed a nearly total absence of the cells that normally give rise to red blood cells. The diagnosis: pure red cell aplasia (PRCA), a disorder seen occasionally in young cats ranging in age from eight months to three years. The cause is believed to be an immune system that has gone a little haywire and attacked the cat's own bone marrow. Aggressive and prolonged treatment with drugs that suppress the immune system is necessary.

We administered the appropriate medications to Tom, and he responded beautifully. His red blood cell count rose steadily. In a few weeks, it was back to normal. We slowly began to taper the medication to the lowest dose that would control his anemia. Meanwhile, Pat and Peter switched from the usual clay litter to a wheat-based litter to dissuade the kitten from further attempts at eating the litter. It seemed to work. Tom showed no craving for the new litter, and he was active and playful.

But several weeks later, Tom suffered a relapse. His gums were pale and his red cell count had plummeted. His owners mentioned that they found Tom licking the silverware, something he had never done before. Fortunately, Tom responded dramatically to an increased dosage of his medications. Interestingly, as soon as Tom's anemia was resolved, the silverware licking ceased.

Pica, the voluntary ingestion of nonedible materials, accounts for approximately 2.5 percent of abnormal behaviors in the domestic cat. Although the cause is unknown, mineral deficiencies or psychological disturbances are often blamed. Tom's unusual ingestive behavior occurred when he was severely anemic. His odd behavior resolved when his anemia came under control. These clues told me that Tom's craving for litter and silverware wasn't simply a mental quirk but had a medical basis behind it.

*Contributed by Arnold Plotnick, DVM*

## TOP REASONS THAT CATS SKIP THE LITTER BOX

(in no particular order)

◆ Dirty litter box

◆ Too few litter boxes for cats in home

◆ Dislike the texture of the litter

◆ New brand of litter used

◆ Household renovations

◆ Move to a new home

◆ New cat, dog, or person added to the household

◆ Change in owner's schedule

◆ Threats from outside cat

◆ Medical condition such as urinary tract infection

◆ Physical discomfort in entering and exiting litter box

# Putting a Lid on It

**Q** We have two cats, ages four and five. We are moving to a new place, and I want to use this opportunity to buy new litter boxes. We've always used open-style boxes, but I like the idea of litter boxes with hoods. My cats have never had any issues with using the litter boxes. Will my cats use covered litter boxes?

**A** Litter boxes, like litter, come in many different designs. In addition to the classic shallow open box, there are the newer covered styles, self-cleaning boxes, round-shaped boxes, and boxes that fit into corners. For the décor conscious, there are even litter boxes that tuck inside furniture to make them appear invisible to people. Some even feature doors that cats learn to open and close.

Since your two cats have used the open-style boxes with no issues, I would recommend that you keep your old ones for now and introduce a third with a hood as a test model. Some cats feel more secure using a litter box with a hood because it provides them with more privacy. Hooded types keep more litter in boxes especially when used by cats who like to kick up a fuss while burying their deposits. Covered boxes also make it harder for household dogs to conduct litter box raids.

However, hooded boxes harbor odor. You must be vigilant and scoop them daily and clean them weekly using warm water and mild detergent and let them air-dry. Hooded types may feel a bit cramped for larger cats to get into position and squat without bumping into the sides or hitting their heads.

If you're willing to perform daily scoop patrol, than introduce the hooded type and let your cats choose. You might find that over time you are able to replace the old boxes with new covered ones.

# Location, Location, Location

**Q** We have a two-story home with three bedrooms and three bathrooms. We also have an enclosed patio. We have two indoor cats, ages fourteen and seven. I want to put the litter box in the master bathroom where I can easily clean it, but my husband insists that it belongs in the basement. Where is the best place in the house to locate a litter box?

**A** Make that litter *boxes.* Veterinarians and animal behaviorists recommend this litter box equation: one litter box per cat plus one extra. In your case, that number is three. Giving your cats choices increases the likelihood that they will routinely use a box instead of choosing a corner of the living room. If one cat stakes out a particular box, the other cat still has a place to go.

Another cardinal rule is to locate a litter box on each level of your home. You want to make litter boxes easily accessible to ensure that they will be used. In your situation, your older cat may have difficulty going up and down stairs. He needs — and deserves — to have a feline bathroom that is convenient to reach on every floor.

As for where, think like a furry realtor for a moment. With cats, it is all about location, location, location when it comes to litter boxes. Cats like their litter boxes in quiet locales that provide them with privacy. In your home, that could mean a corner in your enclosed patio, inside a den, and in the master bathroom as you suggest. Resist stashing litter boxes in laundry rooms or dark, damp basements. Sure, they are out of sight, out of mind for you, but your cats might find these places to be noisy and scary. And the less convenient they are for cleaning, the less likely you are to make a regular habit of scooping the poop.

Never place litter boxes near food and water bowls. It is a common misconception that this placement will serve as a reminder to cats to use the bathroom after meals. You are more likely to stir up a litter box boycott, because cats do not like to relieve themselves where they dine and drink.

## STARTING FROM SCRATCH

Very often, the reason a cat is not using a litter box is because of a medical or physical condition. A urinary tract or bladder infection, an injury, intestinal parasites — there are many causes. If a cat experiences pain while urinating or eliminating, he may associate the box itself with the pain and go elsewhere in an attempt to find a more comfortable spot. Whenever a cat displays a change in elimination habits, the first thing the owner should do is make an appointment for a thorough veterinary exam to rule out any physical problems. Heed this advice: if your cat is unable to urinate for more than two days, contact your veterinarian pronto. This is a life-threatening emergency because after two days of not urinating, a cat can die from kidney shutdown.

Finally, position the litter boxes so they offer a welcoming entrance and escape route. This is important to prevent a cat using a litter box from being startled or tormented by a second cat or visiting dogs or guests. Be sure to escort your kitties to each new litter box location so they are aware of their bathroom options.

And one more tip: if you have dogs, especially those bent on sneaking a "snack" from a litter box, place a baby gate across the doorway to the room containing the litter box. I use a gate with vertical bars and position it about six inches above the floor. My cats have the option of leaping over or slinking under the gate, and it keeps my 60-pound dog, Chipper, from making any surprise visits. Vertical bars are better than horizontal ones that might serve to help a smart dog scramble up and over the gate.

# New House, New Problem

**Q** I have a three-year-old, neutered, domestic short-hair named Winston. My husband and I recently moved from a two-bedroom condo to a four-bedroom detached house. I noticed no urine in the litter pan, so I started looking and found that Winston had urinated on an unpacked box in a spare room. We moved a mattress down to the basement so we could have something to sit on until we get a couch, and Winston urinated on that as well. The problem is, we are ordering a new couch. How can we make sure he doesn't urinate on it?

**A** Cats behave like the Zorros of the companion-animal world. They like to leave their mark on their home turf. Most of the time, they do this by rubbing scent glands from their feet, cheeks, face, and tail on various places inside the home. But sometimes they mark with urine to proclaim ownership or to communicate to other cats within the household or to those lurking outside the back door.

Indoor cats protect their territory just as carefully as outdoor ones. Home represents a place of safety and comfort. Cats also crave routine and abhor change. It is not unusual for a cat in a new home to react by "forgetting"

his previous toileting habits. Winston is doing what comes naturally to a nervous cat — he is marking his new territory with his scent as a way to feel more at home. The items you mentioned contain familiar smells from your condo that Winston misses, and to boost his confidence, he may feel the need to reinforce his markings on them.

Veterinary studies identify several common causes behind urine marking: interactions with other cats outside the home, interactions with cats inside the home, limited access to the outdoors, relocation to a new home, and changes in an owner's daily schedule.

Although cats of either gender will urine mark, intact males are most likely to do so. They use their strong and pungent urine as a way to attract females in the surrounding area. Fortunately, your cat has been neutered, which tones down the odor.

Please rule out any possible medical condition that may be responsible for Winston's changes in bathroom habits. If he is healthy, then the next strategy is to make your new home more welcoming to Winston.

Start by providing new litter boxes and fresh litter. Clean the litter boxes daily. Limit Winston's access to various parts of the new house when you are not at home and definitely make the basement off-limits. Do not yell or hit Winston. You will only elevate his stress and probably prompt him to perform more marking. As he becomes comfortable in his new territory, you can gradually increase his access to the rest of the house.

Urine contains pheromones that communicate a cat's health and mood. There is a product called Feliway that has been demonstrated to be effective in curbing behavior-related urine marking. Feliway is a chemical version of the feline facial pheromone. It works because cats tend not to urine mark locations where they have already left their facial pheromones.

This product comes in a spray as well as a diffuser that plugs into an electric outlet. The diffuser emits this synthetic scent (humans can't smell it) 24 hours a day and lasts for about one month. You can spray Feliway directly onto urine marks and household items such as sofas, drapes, and doorframes without worrying that it will cause a stain.

In extreme cases, urine-marking cats may need calming medications for a period of time. Studies have shown that these drugs can reduce incidents of urine marking up to 75 percent. I urge you to work closely with your veterinarian in administering these medications and then gradually weaning your cat off of them.

We are fortunate that we have many more "weapons" available today than a decade ago to counter urine marking, but it still requires patience, consistency, and compliance with veterinarian's or behaviorist's recommendations to ensure success.

## IS IT SPRAYING OR MARKING?

The terms can be used interchangeably. The only difference is body position and sometimes, the volume of urine that is released.

SPRAYING occurs when a cat backs up to a vertical surface and squirts urine while standing. Both male and female cats will spray, though the behavior is far more common in intact males, who spray as a form of sexual advertising and as a threat to other males.

MARKING happens when a cat squats and urinates on a horizontal surface, such as a bed. This behavior is triggered by emotional stress or general apprehension (from watching their beloved owner pack a suitcase, for example).

Both spraying and marking should be distinguished as behavioral issues. However, keep in mind that some cats avoid the litter box simply because they don't like the location, detest the type of litter (especially citrus scented), or are unable to perform in the litter box due to a health problem.

# Litter Box Avoider

**COCOA, AN EIGHT-YEAR-OLD SIAMESE,** was described by her owner as laid back and comfortable around houseguests. Betty told me that Cocoa was adopted from a humane society when she was about a year old. Betty adored Cocoa's ready purr and cuddling nature but became frustrated and perplexed when Cocoa began defecating outside her litter box and choosing carpeted areas inside the home. The episodes occurred a few times a week.

Medical exams ruled out any physical condition causing Cocoa's change in bathroom behavior. I explained to Betty that some cats defecate outside their litter box as a way of marking their territory. In Cocoa's case, however, considering her relaxed temperament, the reason most likely was due to a preference of surface or material (carpet versus litter box) rather than territorial motivation.

The game plan called for having Betty clean the soiled areas using a bacterial or enzymatic odor-neutralizing cleaner to completely remove the scent of feces, which can be a strong stimulus to return to the same spot. Next, I suggested that Betty keep a journal of the times and places where Cocoa eliminated to aid in choosing the best litter box location.

Betty confessed that she caught Cocoa in the act once and scolded her, causing Cocoa to flee the room. I explained that punishing Cocoa would not stop the unwanted behavior. In fact, it could cause Cocoa to continue this misdeed when Betty was out of sight.

To stop the cycle, I had Betty confine Cocoa in an uncarpeted room with a new litter box for a few days. The room included feline amenities like toys, cat tree, window to view, food, water, and warm bedding. Instead of the hooded litter box Cocoa used, I recommended an open version because some cats don't mind urinating in a hooded box but prefer not to be enclosed when defecating.

Because Betty had a large home, I also urged her to get a second litter box and to fill both with unscented litter instead of the scented type she was currently using. I told her to keep the depth between two and four inches and to scoop the litter box daily. Finally, I had her make the targeted carpeted areas less attractive by attaching contact paper, sticky-side-out, on a piece of cardboard that was placed on top of the carpeted area. She also sprayed citrus scents to deter Cocoa from spending time in those carpeted areas.

With the new litter, open-style boxes, and sticky, citrus-smelling carpet, Cocoa returned to defecating in her litter box on a consistent basis.

*Contributed by Alice Moon-Fanelli, certified applied animal behaviorist*

# My Cat Pees on My Bed

**Q** I jokingly refer to Benny, my three-year-old neutered cat, as Velcro because he follows me from room to room when I am home. He also sleeps on my bed each night, often settling down there before I do. Everything was fine until I adopted a small puppy named Gracie, who is about eight months old and very sweet. Benny hisses at her and doesn't like it when Gracie tries to sleep on the bed at night. On a few occasions, Benny has peed on the bed. What can I do to get Benny to accept Gracie?

**A** Some high-strung cats or solo felines in a home become very attached to their owners. To paraphrase a Shakespearean quote, "Beware of feline jealousy — it is the green-eyed monster." Benny is not about to let a mere mutt muscle in and challenge him as top cat of the household. Since your Pee Prince can't engage in a conversation with Gracie, he tells her in the best way he knows, by marking the disputed territory with his urine.

My advice is to give Gracie her own bed in your bedroom. Motivate her to settle down there by leaving treats on her bed at night. Think of it as a canine version of the mints left on pillows in fancy hotel rooms. You may need to reinforce her new sleeping arrangement by calmly saying "Off" if she jumps on your bed. Usher her back to her own bed and reward her for lying down on it. Gracie should be content with being in the same room as you and her feline mate, Benny.

Reinforce Benny's rank by greeting him first when you come home and feeding him ahead of Gracie. Benny will be definitely paying attention to all of this and will note that Gracie ranks Number 3 in the household. Time is your ally. As Benny sees that this cute pup isn't leaving, but that he still reigns as "top dog" he will become more confident and not need to mark.

I also advise you to keep the bedroom door closed while you're gone and until you go to bed to limit Benny's access. To oust his urine odor from your bedding, clean thoroughly with a protein enzymatic cleaner available at pet supply stores or from your veterinarian.

# Stymied by Stool Situation

**Q** We adopted a healthy 12-week-old kitten. At first, we kept him in the bathroom at night and when we were not at home. He peed in the litter box but pooped in the bathtub. Now that he is older, he has full run of the house. We keep the litter box clean, scooping it every day, but he still poops on the tile floor next to the litter box. I am tired of cleaning it up. What can I do to get him to use the litter box?

**A** The one saving grace is that your kitten is targeting easy-to-clean flooring surfaces rather than carpets or furniture. Having become accustomed to using the smooth tub, he is continuing to find a familiar surface. Your young but savvy kitten is trying to tell you that he is not jazzed by the litter box shape or size, the location, or type of litter. Too often, people forget that litter box usage needs to be addressed from the cat's point of view, not the owner's. Keep in mind that urinating takes less time than defecating. Your kitten may not like to spend a lot of time in the litter box and opt to defecate outside the litter box.

Perhaps the litter box is too small or too large or the litter too deep for his liking. Try adding a second litter box of a different size without a hood. Position this one near the "scene of his poop crimes" but do not put in any litter. Instead, leave it empty or place a liner inside to create a smooth surface to attract your kitten. You may discover that he appreciates this new feline bathroom customized to his liking.

As with all elimination problems, you should have your veterinarian give your kitten a head-to-tail examination to verify that no medical problem exists. Some intact males will do fecal marking to establish their territory, so if you have not done so already, book an appointment to have your kitten neutered. That often cuts down on inappropriate elimination issues and also reduces his risk of developing prostate cancer.

## IDENTIFYING THE CULPRIT

If you share your home with two or more cats and one is boycotting the litter box, how do you identify the culprit?

If your perpetrator is pooping outside the box, give one cat a few drops of red or green food coloring by mouth or in some canned food. His stool will look distinctly more vibrant than those of the other cats. If you have more than two cats, wait a few days and test another cat or give two cats different colors, which is a bit more efficient!

If the issue is urination outside the litter box, ask your veterinarian about an ophthalmic dye called fluorescein that you give orally. Don't worry — it will not harm your cat. At night, you shine a black light around your home for urine spots, which appear as a bright fluorescent tone.

Once you have identified which cat is missing the box, book an appointment with your veterinarian to rule out any possible medical causes for his litter box avoidance before resorting to behavioral tactics described in this section.

# Howling in the Litter Box

**Q** My cat, Billy, has always used his litter box since he was a kitten. He is now nine years old and an indoor cat. There has been no change in the household routine. No recent houseguests, no new furniture, and no changes in what he eats. Lately I have noticed that Billy is making frequent trips to the litter box but producing only small amounts of urine. Sometimes he will squat and nothing comes out, but he howls as if he is in pain. What is happening?

**A** When a well-trained cat suddenly avoids the litter box and there has been no change in the daily routine, the cause is generally medical and not behavioral. Please have Billy checked immediately. He may be suffering from a feline lower urinary tract disease (FLUTD). He is exhibiting the classic signs: frequent bathroom visits, piddles instead of puddles, and pain.

At his age, he may also be at risk for kidney disease, diabetes (especially if he is overweight), hyperthyroidism, or liver disease. These serious medical conditions can make urinating or defecating painful. In addition, arthritis, anal sac disease, and loss of vision may make getting in and out of the litter box difficult. Treatment of these medical conditions may help to resolve this behavioral problem. Also consider adding a couple more litter boxes (try ones with lower sides) and placing the litter boxes in areas where Billy spends the most time. These strategies may be helpful in getting Billy to return to using the litter box normally.

# Toilet-Training Tactics

**Q** I love my cat, Bica, but not her litter box. I hate the smell and the mess, and I hate dealing with the litter. I live in an apartment with a bath-and-a-half, so I have two toilets. I recently started to work from home. I don't want to scoop the litter box every day or clean it every week, and I certainly don't want to be working next to it in my small place. I've read about cats who use the toilet. Bica is a smart, friendly cat, and I think I could teach her to do that. Any advice?

**A** Toilet training a cat is not for everyone — nor every cat. Still, it is easier than you may realize. Some cats can learn in as little as three weeks, but most need a couple of months. The keys are patience and persistence. Training can be messy at first, so you need to keep your bathroom clean for Bica, you, and guests.

Confident and dominant cats make the best bathroom candidates because they tend to deliberately leave their urine and feces uncovered in their litter boxes. Cats with these personalities are more outgoing and willing to learn. Toilet training, however, may prove to be more challenging with shy and submissive cats. In general, these felines prefer to cover their deposits to try to ward off any sign or scent, and they do not embrace changes in the household routine.

Next, do you have what it takes to be a true toilet-training teacher? The chances for success are highest among people who are genuinely interested in their cats, who are sufficiently motivated, and who are very patient. People who don't like to clean the box and who want to save money on litter are the most motivated to learn. That sounds like you.

This tactic works best when you have one bathroom to designate for training your cat and a separate one for you and your guests. You'll have to keep the second bathroom door closed so your cat does not have access to the humans-only bathroom, but always leave the cat-friendly door open.

Before you begin, gather up the following materials: flushable litter, duct tape, plastic litter pan liner or kitchen plastic wrap, litter box, newspapers, and an aluminum roasting pan (12⅝ by 10⅛ by 3 inches deep). Once you have them in hand, follow these recommended steps for toilet training a cat:

1. Post a CAT IN TRAINING sign on the door and a KEEP THE LID UP AT ALL TIMES sign above the toilet.

2. Place the litter box in the bathroom perched on a sturdy three-inch stack of newspapers for five to seven days. Intermittently reward your cat with a food treat when she uses the litter box.

3. Every couple of days, raise the litter box three to five inches with newspapers until the box is even with the closed toilet seat. Your cat may start to walk on the toilet seat. Praise her.

4. Place the litter box on top of the closed toilet lid for a couple of days to accustom your cat to being on top of the toilet.

5. Replace the litter box with the aluminum roasting pan filled with three inches of litter. Put the pan inside the toilet, securing it with duct tape on the sides. Close the toilet seat (not the lid) on top of the pan for a week.

6. Use a screwdriver to make a hole the size of a quarter into the bottom center of the aluminum pan. At this point, sprinkle only a small amount of flushable litter in the pan so as not to clog your toilet. Each day make the hole bigger. After two weeks, cut the entire bottom out of the pan.

7. When the cat is reliably using the toilet, remove the pan and duct tape. Remember to keep the toilet lid up so your cat can balance on the toilet seat. Important: Never flush when the cat is on the toilet!

Proceed slowly and expect some setbacks. If Bica makes a mistake, go back a step for a few days to reinforce the proper behavior. It may seem frustrating, but it is really the only way to overcome resistance to new learning. You also must get in the habit of always leaving the bathroom door open and the toilet lid up to provide 24-hour access for Bica. Otherwise, you risk incurring accidents and behavior problems.

Once Bica has mastered this feat, you can wow your guests by showing off her bathroom talents. And you can delight in never having to change the litter again. By the way, potty-training kits for cats do exist. Some are available from online pet product supply companies.

# **Perplexed by Plastic Preference**

**Q** I have read that cats do not like the feel of plastic. So to stop my cat from peeing on the sofa, bed, and certain areas of the carpet, I put big plastic sheets down. Guess what? She now goes to the bathroom more on the plastic than in the litter box. She will also urinate on plastic grocery bags if they are left empty on the kitchen floor. She is an indoor cat, spayed, about four years old. How can I stop her from peeing on plastic?

**A** Plastic often deters cats from urinating in the wrong places, but your cat is clearly an exception to this rule. Some cats would rather eliminate on a smooth surface than in a pile of litter and will urinate on the bottom of a just-cleaned litter box before owners have time to refill with litter. It has to do with personal feline preference. If you have ruled out a medical reason for not using the box, try providing her with a clean litter box with very little or no litter in it. See Location, Location, Location on page 176 for more on finding the right spot for the litter box.

While you work on making the litter box more acceptable, you need to outsmart your urine-marking cat by putting down other materials that are less appealing. Consider using strips of aluminum foil on the targeted areas. Or, better yet, go to your pet supply store and purchase a double-sided sticky material called Sticky Paws. This ingenious product comes in strips and large sheets and can be applied to places cats should not be. Cats detest the gummy feel on their paws and will soon start avoiding these areas. You can make a homemade version by covering cardboard with contact paper (sticky side out) for the large areas where you don't want your cats to roam. A sheet or large towel sprayed with an aversive scent like Boundary Spray may also be effective.

Don't worry. Your home décor will only be temporarily altered. Most cats will consistently start to steer clear of these areas within a few weeks. You can then remove the deterrents.

# Litter Box Attacks

**Q** I have a sweet, shy Persian named Princess and a bold Abyssinian named Max. I bought Princess first before purchasing Max as a kitten about a year ago. Princess is three. They get along fine until Princess tries to use the litter box. Max seems to enjoy stalking her and pouncing on her when she tries to go. The litter box is located in the corner of a closet in the spare bedroom. I yell at Max, but it doesn't stop him. Poor Princess is becoming a bundle of nerves. She hasn't made any messes outside the litter box, but I'm afraid she may start. Any answers?

**A** Kittens will be kittens, but this is not acceptable. In a multi-cat situation, a dominant cat will pick on a shy cat. Persians by breed tend to be quiet, cuddly, and nonconfrontational. Abys, on the other hand, are more outgoing and bolder. Also, Max is younger and more rambunctious, while Princess has left her silly kitten days behind her.

With the one and only litter box located in a corner of a closet, Princess has no way to flee the scene when attacked. She feels trapped, and you are right to worry that in time she may start secretly urinating behind the couch and other places. The first thing you need to do is add two more litter boxes. The recommended number is one per cat plus one extra. Max cannot guard three litter boxes at one time. With more spots to choose from, he may feel less inclined to protect "his" litter box.

Place the new litter boxes in different rooms. Position them away from walls and in more open areas so Princess can view the room or see the doorway. This will give her a little more time to see Max coming and be better prepared.

Tempting as it is, do not yell at Max. You will only escalate the tension and anxiety that both animals are feeling. Instead, distract Max when you see Princess head to a litter box by engaging him in play or bribing him with a treat. Finally, if you have not already neutered Max, please do so. That will also tone down his bullying tendencies.

## OUSTING ODORS AND STOMPING STAINS

Unfortunately, many household cleaners only temporarily mask the pungent smell of urine, vomit, or feces, which stubbornly fester in your carpet fibers or hardwood floor. But your home need not smell like the local zoo. The sweet smell of success requires a basic understanding of the chemical makeup of urine, feces, and vomit. Composed of organic amines, sulfur, ammonia, and mercaptans, these carbon- and nitrogen-rich compounds attract naturally occurring bacteria in the home. The pungent odors that seem to worsen after using certain household cleaners are the result of volatile by-products created by normal bacterial processes.

Attacking pet messes with household cleaners or homemade solutions containing ammonia or vinegar can worsen the whiff and solidify the stain. Ammonia will actually attract the cat back to the spot. Ammonia is a by-product of urine and using it reinforces the odor rather than removing it. Vinegar acts primarily as a disinfectant and often only temporarily inhibits the environmental bacteria from producing the odor.

Another common mistake is attempting to clean soiled carpeting with a steam cleaner. Steam cleaners work great to remove ordinary dirt, but the heat bakes organic stains into the carpet fibers, leaving a permanent odor.

Timing is key. The faster you can remove fresh urine, vomit, and feces, the fewer odors will be left behind. Poop is fairly easy to scoop with paper towels or a plastic bag, but urine stains are more challenging. Short of replacing the carpet and pad or revarnishing the wood floor, here are a few tips to a sweeter-smelling home.

**SOAK IT UP.** Remove as much urine as possible by blotting it up with paper towels, newspapers, or old cotton rags. Keep pressing on these materials until you no longer see any yellow moisture. Rubbing pushes the urine deeper into the carpet.

**NEUTRALIZE THE ODOR.** Apply a pet-stain enzymatic cleaner to the site. Follow label directions and allow the solution to set before soaking it up by stepping back and forth with paper or cotton towels.

*(continued)*

Be patient. Enzymatic products need at least 24 hours to successfully clean the area. Two highly effective enzymatic cleaners are Nature's Miracle and Zero Odor.

**BRING ON THE BAKING SODA.** For urine-soaked bedding and other machine washable materials, add one pound of baking soda (bicarbonate of soda) along with your detergent and wash with cold water. Baking soda naturally absorbs odors and discourages bacterial growth. Avoid hot water because heat can set the odor in the fabric.

**SPOTTING OLD STAINS.** Old pet messes, especially urine, may be difficult to locate. If you can't pinpoint a particular spot by sniffing it out, buy a black light bulb at your local hardware store. Turn off the lights at night and survey the floor surfaces with this light. Old pet stains give off a greenish-yellow fluorescent glow. Use chalk or other easy-to-clean material to outline the old stain to ensure complete cleanup.

# PART V

# The Basics of Chowing and Grooming

**Cats were born to groom.** Really. In fact, if you recorded a typical 24-hour day in the life of your cat, you would discover that cats spend around one-third of their waking hours fussing over their coats. When was the last time you spent that amount of time styling your hair?

When cats are not grooming or sleeping — or daydreaming about grooming and sleeping — they are eating or thinking about eating. The rest of the time is consumed by finding inviting laps and comfy blankets, toying around with toy mice, and occasionally harassing the family dog for sport.

Perhaps one reason you chose to adopt a cat is because of the feline's fastidious reputation. After all, you never hear someone declare in disgust: Phew! He smells like a cat! Nope, that dis is hurled at dogs — and old socks. You also never hear the term chowcat, even though there are plenty of plump felines who put chowhounds to shame.

In this section, I share some inside secrets about two favorite feline pastimes: grooming and consuming. Read on!

# Saving Face after a Fall from Grace

**Q** I know cats are very agile and possess great balance. So I have to laugh when my cat, Chandler, misjudges the distance of a window ledge, leaps, misses, and falls to the ground. There is not much distance from the ledge to the floor and he never gets hurt. Whenever it happens, he immediately launches into grooming himself. Chandler is a shorthaired black-and-white cat, about four years old. His coat always looks shiny and clean. Why does he groom after he falls?

**A** Cats are dignified critters. While they often act playful or even silly, they are easily discomfited by unexpected events or surprises. Many cat owners notice that their cat will quickly turn away from a startling experience and begin a mini-grooming session. For cats, grooming has important functions beyond health and cleanliness.

The many benefits of grooming began at birth.

Mother cats meticulously clean their kittens. That vigorous licking imparts the power of touch and strengthens the emotional connection between mother and kitten. Littermates and cats that share a household often groom each other as a way to develop their social bond. Grooming also helps cats fend off stress. Veterinary experts report that a cat's heart rate actually slows down during a self-grooming session.

As for Chandler, it doesn't look like he has a future as a tightrope walker for Barnum & Bailey Circus. When cats get caught doing something that startles or surprises them, they instinctively turn to grooming as a way to calm down, collect their thoughts, and restore dignity. It is as if they are saying, "What? I fell? Surely you jest. Why, I'm just making myself look marvelous."

Even though it is hard to resist laughing and pointing at Chandler, try to stifle your giggles. Instead, be his pal by calmly calling him over for a head scratch or a little treat. He will appreciate your gesture.

---

## Groomer to the Rescue

**Q** My cat Zeus is 18 years old. I've had him since he was a kitten. He is a brown-striped tabby with short hair. I've never really thought much about his coat because he seems to keep it clean and tidy. But lately, I've noticed that my other cat, Venus, who is six, has begun to groom Zeus. She licks his head, inside his ears, and even the base of his tail. I thought cats were solitary creatures. Can you explain why Venus is grooming Zeus?

**A** Contrary to the popular but misguided notion that cats are loners, they frequently form close social bonds. Zeus and Venus share the same home, the same

owner. They are part of a harmonious colony. Touch is an important way in which they communicate with one another.

Venus is displaying her affection for her senior friend in the best way she knows how — by assisting him in keeping his coat clean and healthy. In my home, Callie and Murphy do the same for Little Guy (aka Dude), my 19-year-old tabby. Little Guy is not as agile as he was in his youth, and the two younger cats seem to recognize that he is stiffer. So they team up to keep his hard-to-reach areas in tip-top shape. He doesn't protest a bit.

Cats who spend a lot of time together, especially indoor cats who get along, will often engage in this type of "you scratch my back, I'll scratch yours" activity. It solidifies their social bond. This social grooming, known as allogrooming, is common in more than 40 species of animals, including rats, deer, dogs, monkeys, and cattle. In addition to the social aspect, these animals groom one another to treat wounds, tame tensions, and oust bugs such as fleas.

Even though it is sweet that Venus is tending to the grooming needs of Zeus, I urge you to keep tabs on him. If Zeus is not grooming himself at all any more, he may be coping with a medical condition that needs attention. Without Venus stepping in to assist, there is a good chance that Zeus' coat would become dry, dull, and full of dandruff.

### MAT ATTACK!

Conquer mats in longhaired coats by using a wide-toothed comb. Start by carefully pulling apart the mat with your fingers or a mat-splitter as much as you can. Holding the mat at the base, gently but firmly work out the mess by starting at the tip and working in toward the base with the comb. Using scissors sounds like a quick solution, but I advise against it because you risk accidentally cutting your cat's skin. For any mats you cannot comb out on your own, please seek help from a professional cat groomer.

# Create a Glamour Puss

**Q** Our family recently acquired a lovely new cat named Princess, who has beautiful, long, gray fur. I love the longhaired look, but her coat tangles easily and she has several mats on her flanks and belly. I had been assuming that she would groom herself, but I now realize I need to help. I tried to comb her a few times, but I must have tugged too much and she hissed. Now when I approach her with a brush and comb in hand, she glares, runs, and hides. What can I do to make grooming time a more pleasant experience?

**A** Cats usually do a good job of grooming themselves, but they can all benefit from the assistance of a person with a brush. Longhaired cats and cats with very fine, fluffy fur can easily turn into matted, bedraggled ragamuffins without regular, even daily, attention. In the spring and fall, when many cats shed more than usual, a little extra grooming from their human pals helps keep them looking their best.

After your first sessions with Princess, she relates the brush and comb with hair-pulling pain — no wonder she flees from you. And you are probably feeling hesitant and reluctant to approach her, giving her more reason to think that something is wrong. Time to regroup. Have you ever taken a yoga or meditation class? Remember the lessons on deep inhales and exhales from your diaphragm? Be calm and take deep breaths when you are working with Princess. If you are relaxed, she will sense that you don't want to hurt her.

Start your first few grooming sessions by just talking sweetly to Princess and gently stroking her coat from the top of the head to the tail. Move slowly and steadily, and back off if she tries to move away or seems tense. As she relaxes, her purr machine should engage. Use this time to finger gently through her fur for mats, lumps, bumps, cuts, or evidence of fleas. For the first few days, stop your grooming session here. You are rebuilding Princess's trust in you.

For your next sessions, arm yourself with the right tools: a mat-splitter, a wide-toothed comb, and a slicker brush. There are many different brands on the market, but top cat-grooming experts recommend a wide-toothed or shedding comb specifically designed for longhaired cats. The reason? You want to get rid of the dead undercoat hairs that cause tangles.

First remove any mats. Hold the fur between the skin and mat and use the mat-splitter. Your second tool for Princess's belly should be a slicker brush, which will make her coat lie flat. Finish the grooming by lifting the coat away from the body with a wide-toothed comb to add beautiful fullness. (To prevent matting, most longhaired cats with fine coats need to be combed every day taking the comb to the roots.) If Princess's coat is silky and fine, then follow the brush with a grooming glove designed to smooth the coat and cause it to glimmer.

Use flowing strokes on Princess with the wide-toothed comb, moving in the direction of the hair growth. Start at the head and work down toward the tail and then the legs. Take a break and pet Princess and perhaps give her a taste of her favorite treat. If she struggles, let her leave and try again the next day. Don't expect to completely comb out her fur in one session. Be content to attack just one or two mats a day until they are all gone.

Set aside five minutes each day to become your cat's personal groomer. Pick times when you are both relaxed, like in the evenings when you watch television or read a book or in the morning when you wake up and Princess is still a bit sleepy and hungry. Use her empty tummy to your advantage and reward her good grooming behavior with treats. In no time, Princess will look forward to these glamour sessions with you.

If Princess is afflicted with lots of mats or there are any mats too close to the skin for a mat-splitter, you might want to take her to a professional groomer first and get her coat in shipshape condition, then you can follow up with daily at-home care. Don't neglect a longhaired cat — small mats can turn into tough tangles that may need to be shaved off. A final tip: Longhaired cats can greatly benefit from regular bathing since their coats retain body oils and dust, which aggravates the matting problem. A bath also removes dead hair better than combing. Your cat will not only have to become used to the bath process but blow-drying as well. Use of a quiet medium speed, moderate-heat blower works well — most cats eventually come to love the warmth. It is a noisy dryer they dislike.

# Nail Know-How

**Q** When I pick up my cat, she sinks her sharp, long nails into my shoulder and neck. It hurts. Even though she is an indoor cat, I don't plan on having her declawed. How can I keep her nails trimmed and save my skin from her scratches?

**A** My cats Callie and Murphy sport all of their claws and easily accept having their nails clipped on a regular basis. To help you survive nail-trimming time, you need to think like a cat. If given the opportunity, a cat will try to flee the scene. That's why I recommend that you perform this "pet-icure" in a small room like the bathroom. Once a cat scouts the surroundings and realizes there are no escape hatches, she usually complies. And if she doesn't, she'll be easier to catch!

Start by playing with your cat's feet regularly to get her used to someone touching her toes. Gently squeeze the footpads to expose the nails. Do this whenever you are petting her or grooming her.

When you are ready to do an actual trim, set out the tools you will need: nail trimmers designed for cats, a thick towel, and styptic powder (just in case you clip the nail too short and it bleeds). Then bring your cat into the bathroom and give her a small treat to start the proceedings on a good note. Be upbeat. Silly as it sounds, try singing a happy tune. Don't worry if you're off-key — your cat won't tell your friends. Or at least talk soothingly as you work. Sitting on the floor or in a chair, hold your cat with her back against you so that you can hold a paw in one hand and use the clippers with the other.

If your cat struggles too much in this position or tries to scratch, wrap her in a thick towel, exposing her head and her one front paw. Hold the paw steady in one hand. Position your thumb on top of the paw and your other fingers underneath and gently press to expose the nails. Snip the tip of each nail, including the dewclaw on the side. Just nip off the white part, being careful to avoid the vein that runs into each claw.

Tune into your cat's reaction. If she starts to kick up a fuss, then do just one paw this time. You don't want to turn a routine chore into a battle royal. See if a yummy treat will settle her down before you start on the next paw. If she's very upset, wait and do the second paw the next day. Patience is your ally. Depending on your cat, you will need to trim nails every two to four weeks, so make nail-trimming seem ho-hum to your cat.

If you accidentally clip too deep and nick the quick, it will bleed. That's where the styptic powder comes in. Just apply a dab of powder on the nail for a few seconds and apply pressure until the bleeding stops.

Remember to heap on the praise during the trim session. When you are done, open the door and let your cat walk (or run) out. Count to 10 before you leave the room, so your cat won't think you are chasing her. I usually walk out and go in the opposite direction and my cats will stop in the hall, look at me, and begin some spontaneous face grooming to calm down. Within a minute or so, they are following me around as usual.

# Feline Food Fan

**Q** My cat, Emma, acts just like a dog at dinnertime. She persistently begs for food. She works the table, going from one person to the next. Sometimes she even paws at our legs or laps. Mealtime has become a battle of wills. What can I do to enjoy my food and break my pet of her food-begging ways?

**A** Dogs don't have a monopoly on being food beggars, but cats are more coy and mobile. They look at you with their adorable emerald eyes and wink or softly tap your shin with a friendly paw as you prepare to take a forkful of food. Or they deftly land in your lap and begin purring sweetly. You succumb and hand your cat a food morsel from your plate.

See a pattern here? Without realizing it, Emma has "trained" your family to be her personal food servers. Some cats develop their chowhound skills to the point that they reach PhD status (Panhandling for Dinner). Some moochers evolve into bold thieves who will jump up on tables and swipe food off plates. Others develop such a preference for human cuisine that they turn their noses up at the chow you put in their bowls and con you into making them home-cooked meals.

There are two reasons to discourage begging at your table. The first is your peace of mind and the second is your cat's health. If you are having trouble saying no to furry beggars, remind yourself that table scraps are often high in calories and low in nutritional value, especially if you allow Emma to lap up gravy or devour fat from a piece of sirloin. Consuming the wrong food can cause vomiting, diarrhea, obesity, and a host of other health woes.

Healthy treats designed for cats are much better alternatives for snacking between meals, and you can use these food "bribes" to your advantage to reinforce good behavior. However, don't go hog wild on healthy treats either — limit them to about 10 percent of your cat's daily chow.

To put the brakes on begging, implement a new policy of feeding your pets only from their food bowls. If you permit Emma in the dining room at mealtime, the only way to stop her behavior is to ignore it completely. Yelling or pushing her away is not effective and may actually increase her attention-seeking determination. At first, expect her begging behaviors to esca-late, but eventually she will learn that no rewards are forthcoming.

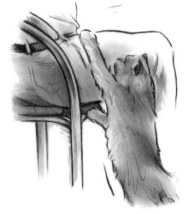

Another solution is to time her meals for when you eat. Feed her in a dif-ferent room where you can close the doors. Keep her there until after the dishes have been cleared from the table. Then open the door and treat her to some calorie-free TLC. Be patient. It will take some time and persistence to introduce this new routine and to stop Emma from pestering you when human food is around.

Naturally, the best advice is not to develop the habit of feeding your cat table scraps in the first place. That way, she will never know what she is missing. And you will ensure that she is more likely to stay at a healthy weight.

## POWER OF PROTEIN

You may wonder if there's a problem with feeding dog food to your cat. The answer is, definitely. Dogs and cats have distinctly different dietary needs. Dog chow lacks certain nutrients that cats need, such as taurine. This amino acid is necessary for the health of cats' eyes, for digesting fats, and for keeping heart muscles healthy. Cats are obligate carnivores and dogs are omnivores. In plain English, that means cats need more meat protein than dogs need. A few nibbles from the dog's dish won't do any harm, but make sure your cat's main meal is kitty kibble, not dog chow.

# Chew on This

**Q** When I head out the door to go to work, I always give my dog a rawhide bone, which seems to keep him happy for the whole day. I tried giving my cat, Garfield (yes, he's big and orange!), a small rawhide bone to chew on. He just sniffed it and ignored it. Why won't he chew on a bone the way Buddy does?

**A** The truth about cats and dogs is that they sport different types of jaw structures. They eat and chew differently. Cats are strict carnivores, whereas dogs are more omnivorous and eat a wider variety of foods. Cats feature sharp, slicing teeth that are designed to snare, hold, and tear apart small prey such as mice and birds. They use their barbed tongues to rasp away bits of meat, rather than relying primarily on their teeth. Feline jaws move up and down, while canine jaws are designed to crush bones and to grind back and forth.

Garfield would probably enjoy that rawhide more if you smeared some cheddar cheese on it and let him lick it clean like a lollipop. In general, cats are fussier about what they stick in their mouths than their kooky canine chums are. That explains why it is easier to fool a dog by hiding his pill in a piece of cheese than it is to fool a cat. Most dogs will gulp down the cheesy treat without hesitation, but most cats will sniff out that disgusting pill and either surgically nibble all the cheese off the pill or saunter out of the room without another glance.

Both dogs and cats have oral fixations. Dogs often pass time and calm themselves down by gnawing on bones. It helps them to relax. Cats often turn to grooming themselves when they feel stressed or unsettled. They like the contact of their barbed tongues on their fur. Grooming is their comfort activity of choice, not gnawing on a disgusting, dog-slobbered bone.

---

# Pass the Greens, Please

**Q** I swear my cat must be part cow! Maggie is a black-and-white cat, about three years old, whom I've had since she was a kitten. She mostly lives indoors, but does go outside, especially when I'm in the backyard. Maggie makes a beeline right for the lawn and starts munching away. Sometimes, she eats a lot only to vomit up the blades of grass later on. Is she okay and why does she seem to like grass?

**A** Your Maggie, though a true carnivore, digs greens. Eating grass is actually a fairly common activity among felines. They have a natural instinct to eat grass and other plants to supplement their dietary needs. Veterinary nutritionists report that an all-meat diet does not provide certain vitamins and minerals that cats seem to know are found in grass and greens.

A second possible reason Maggie heads for the lawn is because the blades of grass serve to help oust hairballs and settle upset stomachs. Yes, the result is a gross puddle (preferably in your yard and not in your house), but Maggie understands the power of Mother Nature.

I caution you to steer Maggie away from the lawn if you use any kind of chemicals or pesticides. Instead, treat Maggie to an indoor patch of organically grown lawn in your house. Grass is easy to grow and it sprouts quickly. Better yet, grow fresh catnip for Maggie. This hardy herb is easy to grow from seeds. Just set the pot in a dark, damp area to allow the seeds to sprout and then relocate the pot to a sunny spot. I recommend a place where Maggie likes to sun herself, perhaps near a window in the living room.

You can also consult your veterinarian about providing Maggie with a commercial hairball preventative. In addition, regular wet-hand grooming can help oust dead hairs in Maggie's coat and may reduce her hairball episodes.

## Finicky Feeder

**Q** I've had cats all my life and have always been able to fill a bowl, walk away, and watch them eat. Easy, right? Not any more. I recently brought in a stray

cat. I'm guessing she is about three years old. I thought she would be grateful to have a home, but she is quite picky about what she eats. My other two cats eat their dry food without any problem. This new cat, Gabby, does love salmon and tuna, but I can't keep catering to her expensive tastes.

**A** While cats have long been branded with a reputation as picky eaters, I prefer to regard them more as discriminating eaters. You need to assess what's going on. Is Gabby really being a picky eater or is something else at play? Grab a notepad and write down Gabby's eating habits over the next few days. There are several possible explanations why Gabby doesn't gobble her kibble. She may be satisfied with treats and table scraps such as those pieces of delicious salmon and tuna you hand out. Or the other two cats may be blocking her from the food bowl. Try setting out another one to lessen the competition. Speaking of bowls, some cats don't like their whiskers touching the sides of food bowls and will walk away from their kibble if the bowl doesn't "fit." Gabby may need a larger or shallower bowl.

The location may also be a turnoff, especially if the food bowl is in a noisy, high-traffic area like the kitchen. Some cats like to dine without a lot of hoopla around them.

Does Gabby spend any time outside? She may have charmed a neighbor into giving her tasty treats or she may be filling up on gophers and sparrows.

Finally, do not rule out a possible medical condition. Gabby may have tender gums or missing teeth that make chewing a challenge.

Cats like routines. If you feed your cats a variety of commercial dry food, Gabby may be holding out in hopes of something tastier than the current kibble. It's better to stick with one brand consistently. You may spice it up a bit by pouring a little broth over the kibble, but once you find a quality cat food Gabby seems to like, stay with it. If her health needs change, switch her gradually to another type of food. I recommend working closely with your veterinarian on the best dietary choice. Good luck!

**FELINE FACT**

Himmy, an Australian cat, is the heaviest cat on record, weighing in at 46 pounds, 15.25 ounces in 1986, according to the *Guinness Book of World Records*.

# Food for Thought

**Q** I'm about to adopt a pair of young cats from the local shelter. They are just a year or two old and are littermates. I don't want my cats to get fat from overeating. Should I just keep a big bowl of kibble available to them all the time or feed them twice a day?

**A** Welcome to the Great Feline Food Debate. There are pros and cons to both free feeding and scheduling specific mealtimes. Many cats, whether they live as solo cats or part of a multi-cat household, seem to fare well with free feeding. They eat what they need and stop before becoming obese. Unlike dogs, who tend to bolt down whatever food is put in front of them, cats are more comfortable nibbling 10 to 20 times a day.

In your situation, I would first check with the animal shelter officials as to how these sibling felines were fed. Ask if they ate twice a day or had food available all day long, and inquire whether there were any incidents of one cat bullying or nudging the other from food bowls.

Keep tabs on your new cats' eating habits and weigh them regularly. If they seem to maintain their weight, then free feeding is a good option. Just be sure to clean the bowls regularly — daily if you feed canned food.

Some cats, however, view free feeding as a 24-hour all-you-can-eat buffet and stuff themselves with kibble until their bellies drag on the floor. They just can't say no to chow. Consider this startling fact: an extra three pounds on a nine-pound cat is the equivalent of adding a whopping 40 extra pounds to a 120-pound person. Added weight puts both cats and people at added health risk.

For cases in which one cat eats too much and one eats too little, scheduling specific mealtimes is recommended. This allows you to have better control over your cats' diets. To prevent the pudgy cat from gobbling up all the food, feed him in a separate room. Then, after a designated time, around 15 minutes or so, pick up the food bowls. Another option is to feed the slender cat an extra meal at night, while the plumper puss spends the night in a room of his own without any food.

Controlled feeding also works best when a medical problem arises, such as diabetes. Cats with this condition need to have their insulin and blood sugar levels monitored on a daily basis. Feeding small amounts a number of times each day can also help a cat who eats too much food at once and may throw up a short time later.

If you find yourself unable to be at home at specific mealtimes for your cats, consider buying a timed self-feeder. These gadgets dispense controlled portions of kibble at designated times. Putting a couple of golf balls in the food dish will also help to slow down a greedy gobbler, as will spreading out the kibble on a tray or shallow dish.

## LACK OF A SWEET TOOTH

Open a can of tuna and watch your cat come running to share your lunch, but bring out a candy bar or a bag of cookies and he is most likely completely indifferent. Most cats are not interested in sweet treats.

All mammals have receptor cells located on their tongues that transmit taste signals to their brains. Human taste buds can detect five major taste sensations: salty, sweet, sour, bitter, and umami, which is a meaty or savory flavor.

Scientists recently discovered that two proteins regulate sweet receptors. In the case of cats, one of these proteins, T1R2, is missing. Cats are at the very least indifferent to sugar and at most unable to detect it.

So, why do some cats beg for a taste of ice cream or yogurt? These dairy products contain a large amount of a protein called casein, which is made of amino acids that cats need in their diets. Dairy products also tend to contain fat, which cats are well suited to digest and utilize.

# Yuck! Hairballs!

**Q** My longhaired cat, Pretty Kitty, seems to groom her beautiful silver coat all the time. She is an indoor-only cat nearing her fifth birthday. At least once or twice a week, I can count on finding a hairball coughed up on the carpet. She never seems to pick floors that are easy to clean, like the tile in the kitchen. She gets regular checkups, and my veterinarian has not found any health problems. So why the hairballs?

**A** Unfortunately, hairballs can be a constant nagging issue for longhaired cats and many shedding short-haired ones as well. Cats normally swallow hair when they groom. The tiny barbs on their tongue act like a hairbrush, grabbing loose hair. Most of the time, this swallowed hair passes through the digestive system without incident.

However, when cats have a lot of hair to begin with or are shedding, swallowed hair accumulates in the stomach where it can irritate the stomach lining and interfere with digestion. Once the hairball reaches a certain size, the cat vomits to expel a messy wad of hair, digested food, saliva, and gastric secretions — the ingredients of your typical feline hairball. Yuck!

I urge you to consult with your veterinarian again if the number of hairball incidents increases or if your cat appears to be in discomfort when she vomits. A radiograph may be necessary to determine if a hairball is stuck in her stomach. In some cases, impacted hairballs must be surgically removed.

Even though Pretty Kitty is quite a fastidious groomer, you can help reduce the hairball incidents by brushing and combing her daily. Grooming also aids in spotting any skin or coat problems such as lumps, bumps, and fleas, removes dead skin, and minimizes matting. Your clothing and furniture will benefit, too, because there will be less flyaway cat hair circulating in your house. You can also treat her to an appointment at a pet-grooming salon on a regular basis.

Another way to combat hairballs is to feed your cat a petroleum-based lubricant, available from your veterinarian or at most pet supply stores. Some cats tolerate straight Vaseline, but many don't like the taste. Whichever brand you use, dab a bit on your cat's nose or paw. She will automatically lick that area and ingest the lubricant. Most of these are flavored to encourage cats to view them as a treat. Do not use butter or vegetable oil as they are high in calories and not absorbed efficiently by cats. Virgin olive oil can be used sparingly.

> **FELINE FACT**
> Hairball is such a yucky word. The scientific name for that hacked-up mess is "trichobezoar."

Why the carpet and not the tile floor? That remains one of the feline mysteries in life. My home is mostly laminate and tile, but whenever my cats have upset tummies, they too leave the evidence on the only carpeted area of my house — my bedroom and upstairs hallway.

# Amber Overgrooms Herself

AMBER, AN 11-YEAR-OLD SPAYED DOMESTIC SHORTHAIR, had lived with Sylvia since the age of eight weeks. This indoor-only cat always sported a clean, shiny, well-groomed coat. Although she dashed out of view any time the doorbell rang, Amber enjoyed hanging around Sylvia's boyfriend when he visited.

About a year ago, Amber's feline housemate, Pookie, became very sick and had to be euthanized. Sylvia told me that Amber watched her put Pookie in the carrier and leave the house and return home without Pookie. After her companion's death, Amber started to excessively lick her abdomen and hind legs. She also began to lose weight, even though Sylvia did not make any changes in her diet.

Working with her veterinarian, Sylvia ruled out any medical conditions and possible allergic reactions to parasites, food, dust, pollen, or mold. I informed Sylvia that Amber was suffering from what is known as psychogenic alopecia. Cats normally groom as a displacement behavior when momentarily stressed, but in some cases, the frequency and duration of the sessions last longer than is considered functional. When exacerbated by stress, grooming can become repetitive and excessive, sometimes resulting in bald patches and self-chewing bite marks on the skin.

In general, psychogenic alopecia occurs more often in females than males, and it can happen at any age. It is seen predominantly, but not exclusively, in pedigreed cats of Oriental breeding and is usually associated with cats who have anxious temperaments. Clearly, Amber missed Pookie. The other cat in the home, Honey Boy, behaved like a bully, so I advised Sylvia to fit his collar with a bell so that Amber could be forewarned of his whereabouts and avoid a confrontation.

I recommended that Sylvia engage Amber in five to ten minutes of interactive exercise and play a couple of times each day. Feather toys, catnip mice, and crinkly objects are favorites with many cats. Enriching the environment with a feline hammock for the cats to climb on and giving them treat balls to play with helped calm and distract Honey Boy, which decreased Amber's anxiety.

As an interim measure, I also suggested that Sylvia consult with her veterinarian about temporarily administering a calming medication used to treat compulsive disorders such as psychogenic alopecia. Amber's grooming behavior was reduced and her coat regained its shiny, healthy look.

*Contributed by Alice Moon-Fanelli, certified applied animal behaviorist*

---

**SOURED BY MILK?**

Even though many people think cats and milk go together like mice and cheese, veterinarians generally advise against treating your cat to a big saucer of milk. Adult cats do not produce enough of the enzyme lactase to properly digest the lactose found in milk. Even a few table-spoons of milk can cause diarrhea or vomiting. Why take the chance?

---

# Tubby Tabby Weighs In

**Q** I love my big huggable cat, Leo, but my friends joke about his size. They call him Leo the Large and ask me if I really have two cats, not one. He is eight years old and weighs 16 pounds. I tell my friends he is just big-boned, but I know he is overweight. He doesn't seem to have any health problems, however. What's wrong with having a chubby cat?

**A** Plenty. I know from experience. My youngest cat, Murphy, was always the athletic one of my feline trio until a few years ago. Each morning, I would take her for a walk in my neighborhood. She would come running to the door when I brought out the leash and harness. Then I added a dog to the family, and then another. Instead of taking Murphy for a walk or tossing a paper wad down the long hallway for her to fetch, I started walking and running with my canines.

Murphy sat home and ate and ate. Kibble by kibble and treat by treat, she packed on the ounces until she reached 15 pounds. Like you, I had to come to grips with my part in creating a fat cat. Unfortunately, you and I are not alone. Up to 40 percent of all cats in the United States tip the scales as overweight or obese.

Overweight cats are at increased risk for diabetes, heart disease, arthritis, and a host of other conditions. As their bellies expand, they are less motivated to do anything beyond eating, sleeping, and making the occasional trip to the litter box. They often drink less water, which makes them likelier candidates for stones in their urine or for urinary tract infections.

Let's help Leo slim down smartly. Take a "before" photo of him and put it in a visible place such as your refrigerator door. Start a food diary and weigh Leo once every three days. If you keep his food bowl always full, cease. Ask you veterinarian for advice on a high-quality diet food (some have more fiber, which helps the cat feel fuller) and slowly wean him from his regular food to the lower calorie version. Set up specific mealtimes and measure each portion according to the directions on the package. Use an actual measuring cup, not a plastic deli container or other imprecise scoop. Spread out his kibble on a cookie sheet instead of a bowl. It will take him longer to eat his chow.

Work with your veterinarian on slowly decreasing Leo's food portions. You don't want to cut back too quickly. In cats, the dangers of "crash dieting" can lead to hepatic lipidosis, more commonly known as fatty liver disease.

Your goal is for Leo to lose a few ounces per week, so that the excess weight comes off gradually and doesn't return. As the ounces start to melt, bring out the inner kitten in Leo by encouraging him to play and move around more. If you have stairs, put a low-calorie treat like shaved bonito fish flakes at the top of the stairs when Leo is at the bottom. Show him the treat and call him up. Drag a toy on a string for him to chase. Buy him an interactive toy that will engage his attention when you are away.

Take monthly progress photos of Leo. Within six months or so, your friends will be calling him Leo the Lean.

> ## FUTURE FAT FIGHTER?
>
> Veterinary nutritionists are studying the possible benefits that L-carnitine may hold for increasing fat metabolism when added to cat food. They are also looking into different types of fiber. L-carnitine (short for levocarnitine) is an amino acid nutrient that may help decrease the levels of cholesterol and lipids (fats) in the blood. This supplement is available in pet supply catalogs and stores. As with any supplement, talk to your veterinarian before adding it to your cat's diet.

# Bath? No, Thanks

**Q** My dog, Max, is a gentle Bull Mastiff who loves to swim and take baths. My cat, Star, definitely resists getting wet. I have to bathe her occasionally, though, because Max tends to slobber on her and she smells like a dog. Why do cats hate baths so much?

**A** Cats are extremely conscious of hygiene. If they were people, they would probably be labeled obsessive-compulsive because they would be washing their hands numerous times a day. They would never be caught in public wearing a dirty T-shirt or clothes that clashed. They like sporting clean, well-groomed coats. That must be why cats with black-and-white coats are fondly referred to as tuxedo cats — not Oreo cookie cats.

While an encounter with a skunk or some sticky or oily substance does necessitate human intervention, most cats never need to be bathed at all. A good brushing (daily for fluffy felines and less frequently for shorter-coated cats) helps keep skin and fur healthy. Unless Star is regularly drenched with dog drool, let her take care of the problem herself with self-grooming. If she is still stinky, try using a dry or mousse shampoo or unscented, alcohol-free wipes rather than subjecting her to a full-fledged bath.

If you do feel that she needs to be bathed, start with room-temperature water in a sink or tub, only on the feet at first. Use a cup to pour water over the back (the faucet can be frightening), give a gentle massage, towel dry, and let the cat go. Accustom your cat to short sessions with no shampoo at first, then gradually add a quick foamy shampoo massage and a thorough rinse.

As for the notion that *all* cats take to water like oil to vinegar, that statement does not in fact hold water. Some wild felines, like tigers and ocelots, may cool down from the jungle heat by swimming, or enter water to hunt fish and other aquatic creatures. Corky, my childhood cat, loved to swim with our dogs in our backyard lake and would follow anyone holding a fishing pole in hopes of landing a bluegill dinner. Many domestic cats are fascinated with water even if they don't like to swim, and some come to enjoy regular baths. (See questions in part III.) I've seen several cats looking quite happy aboard fishing boats in southern California harbors, though admittedly, they are not actually in the water!

---

# Uh-oh, It's Pill Time!

**Q** The vet determined during our last visit that my cat, Cosmo, must take pills twice a day for an ongoing medical condition. I know that the medicine will make him feel better, but it is becoming more difficult to administer the pills. He seems to have a sixth sense about when I plan to give him medicine, and then he runs and hides. How can he know it is pill time?

**A** For one thing, cats are creatures of habit, so if you have been giving Cosmo his pill at a regular time, he has come to expect that you will "attack" him, as he sees it, at the same time every day. He is also probably associating the rattle of the pill bottle with the unpleasant event. Cats are also quite adept at gauging our emotions. It sounds as though you are stressed and frustrated when it is time to give Cosmo his pills. He studies your body language, sees the tension building in your muscles, and knows exactly what is coming next.

Giving medicine to our pets will never rank among our favorite activities, but remind yourself that you are doing a great job of taking care of your cat. Up to 40 percent of pet owners fail to comply with their veterinarians' instructions on medicating their pets. The main reason? It's too much of a hassle.

**FELINE FACT**
Feline eyes come in three shapes: almond, round, and slanted.

Since you must give pills to Cosmo twice a day, try stashing the bottle in a place he likes to hang out, like next to your sofa or favorite recliner or in the nightstand by your bed. Take the pill from the bottle and wait a bit. Let Cosmo come to you. Help him relax — and you, too — by treating him to a therapeutic massage. Listen for his purr machine to engage and his body to relax. Then quietly grab the pill and, while still speaking sweetly, calmly, and confidently, open his mouth and pop in the pill, making sure to place it far enough back in his throat that he can't spit it out. Hold his mouth closed for a moment and gently stroke his throat to make sure he swallows.

If that isn't feasible, here is Plan B: Motivate your cat to come to you at pill-dispensing time by associating a favorite treat (we're talking Grade-A level, like canned tuna, not stale kibble) with the rattle of the pill bottle. Reward him for coming to you. Without making rushed movements, pick him up and pop in the pill — or sit on the floor so you can better hold him. You may need to wrap him in a towel to keep him from scratching you.

And then there is Plan C: This works more for dogs than cats, but there are always feline exceptions. You can try grinding the pill into a powder, concealing it in a tablespoon of canned food or meat baby food, or rolling it into a glob of cheese. Some cats love vitamin supplements or hairball remedies in a tube, and a dab of this, hiding the medication, can be put on the roof of the mouth, where it will stick. Please check with your veterinarian first, however, to make sure that pulverizing the pill won't affect its potency.

Whichever option you choose, speak in upbeat tones and remember to breathe in and out deeply to keep your body from tensing. If Cosmo scoots away after the pill time, ignore him and walk in the opposite direction or stay put and read or watch TV. You want to communicate to him that pill time is not a big deal.

# Pumpkin,
# a Plastic-Loving Cat

WHEN OWNERS REPORT THAT THEIR CAT IS VOMITING, I must do a little detective work to make an accurate diagnosis. In this case, Pumpkin's owner made my job easier when she declared, "Pumpkin likes to eat plastic, especially those plastic grocery bags from the corner deli."

Armed with this information, Pumpkin and I took a little trip to the X-ray table. Plastic bags, unfortunately, are radiolucent, which means they don't show up well on X-rays. However, I could see on Pumpkin's X-ray an abnormal gas pattern in the intestine and something not right in his abdomen. The verdict: Pumpkin most likely swallowed something that was obstructing his intestinal tract. Any food that he ate was unable to move past the obstruction and was forced back out.

The smell of the vomit suggested that the obstruction was far enough along in the intestinal tract for the food to be in the process of being transformed into poop when it hit the obstruction and came back out. I mention this not to gross you out but to illustrate that sometimes a seemingly trivial observation — the vomit smelled awful — can yield important clues for veterinarians.

Pumpkin was admitted to our hospital, rehydrated with intravenous fluids, and given preoperative antibiotics. During exploratory surgery, one section of the intestine was inflamed with a telltale bulge. I made my incision and spotted a shredded plastic grocery bag. Then I noticed two other smaller pieces of plastic, which turned out to be proof-of-purchase coupons cut out from a package of disposable diapers.

What is it about plastic bags that entice cats? Some speculate that cats like the coolness, the texture on their tongue, or the sound it makes when they lick or touch it. The most logical reason I've heard is that cats do this because gelatin is utilized during the manufacture of some plastic bags. Gelatin is an animal product, and some cats are attracted to the gelatin smell. Although this is still a theory, it makes sense to me.

Pumpkin's case is an excellent example of how a behavioral issue — a crazy craving for plastic — can lead to a potentially dangerous medical condition: gastrointestinal obstruction. Pumpkin's owner may want to consider old-fashioned cloth diapers for her next baby.

*Contributed by Arnold Plotnick, DVM*

**A SPOONFUL OF SUGAR (OR TUNA)**

Who said medicine must taste bad to do good? Check with your veterinarian about compounding your cat's pills into flavored, easily administered liquids instead. Pharmaceutical companies now offer a dozen or so feline-friendly flavors such as grilled tuna, roast lamb, and Angus beef for more than 350 veterinary prescriptions.

In addition, the companies can take the bitterness out of medicines like metronidazole or prednisolone while maintaining their potency. Some medications for hyperthyroidism can be made into transdermal gels that can be massaged into the tip of your cat's ear to be absorbed through the skin rather than swallowed.

# Taking It under the Chin

**Q** I was scratching my three-year-old cat, William, under his chin recently when I felt some scabby bumps and noticed flakes of what looked like dirt. I know he doesn't have fleas, and he's always taken good care of his coat. I was afraid that he might have mange or even skin cancer, but my veterinarian diagnosed it as feline acne. I've never heard of this condition. Can you tell me more about it?

**A** Teenagers aren't the only ones who develop acne — some cats do, too. Medically speaking, feline acne is a keratinization disorder, which is a fancy way of saying that pores under the chin become blocked with cellular debris, causing blackheads. Left untreated, these clogged pores can become swollen and infected. They eventually rupture and create bloodied scabs, raised lesions, and patches of baldness. Cats with white chins may look like they have goatees.

**FELINE FACT**
The main reasons for a cat to develop itchy skin are allergic reactions, fleas and other parasites, diseases such as diabetes and hyperthyroidism, dry environment, poor diet, poor grooming, and bacterial or fungal infections.

Veterinary experts do not know what causes this condition or how prevalent it is among the feline population. Popular theories point to heightened stress, use of plastic feeding bowls, fleabites, a genetic predisposition, or allergies as possible triggers. Feline acne can appear just once and disappear forever or it can last for the cat's entire lifetime.

Keeping a case of feline acne under control requires working closely with your veterinarian and possibly a veterinary dermatologist. There are a variety of treatments available, from over-the-counter ointments to prescription medications, but the trick is finding which one works best on your cat. Here are a few common treatments:

**FLEA COMB.** Run the comb gently under the chin on a daily basis to lift and remove dried scabs and blackhead flecks.

**MEDICATED ACNE PAD.** Dab your cat's chin once or twice a day to keep the blackheads on the chin from worsening. Let the area air-dry.

**EPSOM SALT COMPRESS.** Hold a warm compress on the chin for three to five minutes a day to dry out the area and reduce inflammation. Then apply Vitamin A ointment to repair damaged skin cells.

**PRESCRIPTION SHAMPOO.** Apply this with warm compresses to cleanse and exfoliate dead skin in the chin area. Check with your veterinarian for dosage instructions.

**BENZOYL PEROXIDE GEL.** This prescription medication typically contains 2.5 to 3 percent benzoyl peroxide that penetrates deeply into the hair follicles to remove blackheads. Caution: the peroxide can bleach fabric if the treated cat rubs his chin against the furniture or carpeting.

**ORAL ANTIBIOTICS.** Given in pill or liquid form, medication may be prescribed if the acne becomes infected.

My veterinarian friends offer one final bit of advice: Do not squeeze any pimple under your cat's chin — you risk causing an infection.

## PETTING WITH A PURPOSE

One of the best ways to communicate with our cats is through touch. Most cats love to be stroked, petted, and scratched. Most people enjoy the feel of that silky fur and the sight of a happy, purring face. When properly performed, the power of touch delivers many therapeutic and health benefits.

One of the best ways to touch is through massage. Daily massages can help you detect fleas

*(continued)*

or ticks. You can also look for cuts or suspicious lumps. Massage can play a role in chronic conditions such as arthritis. Although not a cure, gentle massage reduces joint stiffness and pain by delivering oxygenated blood to those trouble spots.

Massage strengthens the people–pet bond, helps curb aggression and other unwanted behaviors, and improves a cat's sociability with people and animals. Another advantage is that regularly massaged cats become accustomed to being handled. They associate touch with positive experiences. That can take the stress out of combing and brushing, nail trimming, car trips, veterinarian visits, and cat breed shows for both the cat and the owner.

Start with a basic massage stroke known as "effleurage." This French word means "to flow or glide" or "skim the surface." Effleurage is always performed toward the heart in the direction of the venous blood flow, which helps remove wastes and toxins and refresh the tissues and muscles. On a cat's legs, for example, work from the toes toward the knees and hips.

Here are some suggestions:

**GO WITH THE GLIDE.** This classic massage stroke is simply a straight, flowing, continuous motion. Move your fingers or palm from the top of the head down the back to the tail.

**CREATE CIRCLES.** Move your fingertips in clockwise or counterclockwise circles about the size of half-dollars.

**DO THE WAVE.** Make side-to-side rocking strokes with open palm and flat fingers (mimic the movements of a windshield wiper).

**FOCUS ON FLICKING.** Pretend that you are lightly brushing imaginary crumbs off a table. You can flick with one, two, or three fingers.

**USE THE REAL RUB.** Move along your cat's body slowly, exerting feather light, light, and mild pressures. See which she responds to best.

**HEED THE KNEAD.** This gentle caress uses an open-and-shut motion of your palm and all five fingers. It is ideal for the spine area.

*(continued)*

And some final suggestions for a massage session that is soothing and satisfying for both you and your cat:

- Do approach your cat slowly and speak in a soothing tone.
- Don't force a massage on your cat.
- Don't massage your cat when you feel stressed or hurried.
- Do use clean hands — no need for oils, creams, or lotions.
- Do pay attention to feedback. Look for purring, rolling on to one side, kneading, and soft eye blinking. Stop your massage if your cat squirms away from you, hisses, sinks his back under your hand, or meows in protest.
- Don't press too deeply — you could harm your cat.
- Don't try to substitute massage for medical treatment for conditions such as arthritis. Let it complement the care plan devised by your veterinarian.

# PART VI

# The Ins and Outs of Living with Cats

**Is your cat part of** the "in" crowd? By that, I don't mean is he a cool cat, but is he a safe cat? Safe cats live indoors and do not roam outside without supervision.

Times have changed. A generation ago, most household cats freely wandered wherever their curiosity steered them. My childhood cat, Corky, used to stay out all night until he limped home with a gaping wound from the fan blade of a car. He found a warm spot to snooze by climbing inside the engine. That was the last time that he spent any solo time outside.

Cats still stalk the outdoors, but many people choose to keep their feline friends inside. Cats can live happily inside, enjoying the view out the windows, climbing on special cat trees, and playing with a variety of boredom-busting toys. Do you choose freedom or safety? The choice is yours, but now you know my views.

Paw through this section with an open mind. Find new ways to make your home truly fit for your feline. And if your cat drives you crazy, look for answers to sharing your bed, teaching an old cat new tricks, and traveling with (or without) your pal.

# Pillow-Hogging Puss

**Q** My kitty, Bebe, is adventurous and adoring by day but turns into a pillow pig at night. At bedtime, she starts out at the foot of my bed while I brush my teeth. When I crawl under the covers, she creeps forward and nestles by my side. But by the middle of the night when I am in a deep sleep, she has commandeered my pillow. She walks right over me and wakes me up. I like having her sleep on my bed, but how can I keep her off my pillow so I can get some sleep?

**A** When it comes to sharing your bed with your cat, you're not alone. About one-third of today's cat owners sleep with their felines. Little wonder. Their furry bodies and soothing purrs often help lull people to sleep. A study conducted at the Mayo Clinic Sleep Disorders

Center, however, found that about half the people who let pets share their bed at night suffer from disrupted sleep that results in their being tired each morning. The researchers also found that many people are so attached to their pets that they are willing to tolerate poor sleep in order to be near them at night.

I have to admit that I'm guilty — my cats stay down at the bottom third of my bed, but I sleep on my back, an ideal position for cats who wish to snooze with their heads propped on ankles or calves. Fortunately, I'm a heavy sleeper and my cats are, too. Once they carve out a spot, they tend to sleep until morning.

In your case, however, Bebe sounds like one bossy cat. She feels entitled to sleep wherever she chooses, regardless of your preferences. Cute as she may be, you need to regain control of your bed and your pillow and retrain Bebe about bed boundaries. Start by making the bottom of your bed more appealing. Provide Bebe with her own plush pillow or soft fleecy blanket. Praise her when she settles down there. Be consistent about moving her to the bottom of your bed before you are asleep. Or compromise by providing Bebe with her own pillow next to yours.

To make your pillow less appealing, consider lightly spraying your pillow with a citrus scent (one you enjoy). Cats are not fond of that aroma. If she wakes you up in the middle of the night, either put her back in her spot or push her on to the floor. After being ousted a few times, most cats get the idea and adjust to the new bedroom rules.

You may sacrifice a few nights of sleep to teach Bebe about the new no-pillow zone, but she will soon realize she has a great spot at the foot of your bed. Sweet dreams!

## SLEEPLESS IN SAN DIEGO

On any given night, Bob Walker and Frances Mooney share their double bed with as many as eight cats in their San Diego home. (See page 272 for more on this couple's extremely cat-friendly accommodations.)

Walker says he usually sleeps on his stomach and a cat always shares his pillow. He has been known to make contortionist movements so as not to disturb sleeping feline on his legs.

When told about the findings of the Mayo Clinic study on how pets can contribute to insomnia, he took it in stride. "What's a little lost sleep if you can keep your cats happy?" he asks. "I can't remember the last time that I got eight hours of uninterrupted sleep. To me, you're not a true cat lover if you can sleep soundly."

# **Ahh, the Great Indoors**

**Q** My cat, Bruno, is a big, muscular cat. He is very friendly and easygoing. Since he was a kitten, he has ventured wherever he pleased around the neighborhood. Our property is one acre with some woods. Bruno is now 10 years old and seems to be slowing down a bit. Our winters here are cold and nasty. The addition of a recent housing development in our neighborhood has created more traffic on our street. For all these reasons, I'd like Bruno to become an indoor cat. What's the best way for me to do this without upsetting him?

**A** You certainly don't want a Bruno protest. Remind yourself that your actions are done out of genuine love and concern for Bruno. You are giving Bruno the best gift you can give him — a longer, healthier life.

I can tell you have already assessed the "feline fear factor." You recognize that Bruno's age plus worsening weather and escalating traffic are increasing the chance of his becoming injured or ill due to his free-roaming lifestyle. With Bruno indoors, you will no longer have to worry about him developing an abscess from scrapping with a stray, being exposed to poisonous yard-care products or antifreeze, or developing a contagious disease like feline leukemia.

It's only natural to feel a little guilt at first. You are probably assuming that Bruno will feel that his freedom has been yanked from him. He may indeed act out in undesirable ways, like urine marking, yowling at the door, or clawing your sofa.

To avoid these bad behaviors, you need to make his indoor domain far more stimulating and appealing than the outside scene that he is used to. An outdoor cat exercises more and engages his senses more, so you will need to replace the sights, smells, and sounds of the outdoors. Bruno may be 10 years old, but he probably has a lot of kittenish play left in him. He needs daily exercise and interactive play sessions to keep him happy and not pining for the outdoor life. Catnip mice, cat wands, and feather toys on sticks can all be used to bring out the playful predator in Bruno and give him appropriate outlets for hunting, stalking, and chasing. Look for toys that he can play with by himself, such as a ball in a round track or a mouse on an elastic string that you hang in a doorway. Put some kibble in a hollow toy that he can bat around so that treats trickle out.

If he shows any interest in watching your television, you could buy him a couple of nature programs specially designed to engage the attention of cats. Provide Bruno with suitable places to scratch and claw and a comfy perch to view what's happening outside. Position some sturdy scratching posts in key rooms where the two of you spend a lot of time, such as the living room and bedroom. Install a window perch that overlooks a bird feeder or a tree where the local squirrel gang likes to hang out.

The latest trend in feline décor is outdoor enclosures that allow a cat to safely enjoy a bit of the outdoors without coming to any harm. Cat fencing is also available. (See Bring the Outdoors In, page 268.)

If Bruno starts making loud demands at the door, your natural instinct may be to yell at him to quiet down. That won't work. You two will only get in a "who can yell louder" match. And guess what? You'll lose. Instead, ignore him. It won't be easy initially and your patience will be tested. When he is quiet for even a few seconds, call him over and give him a treat or scratch his chin or play a game with him. In time, his yowling will subside as he realizes you are not caving in to his demands.

I want to address the issue of inappropriate elimination, which can be a problem for a cat making the transition to indoor life. If Bruno has traditionally performed his bathroom duties outside, you may need to teach him how to use a litter box. I recommend that you confine Bruno to a small but cozy room for a week or so. Provide him with a litter box that you scoop out daily. Locate his bed and his food and water bowls on the opposite side of the room from the box. Ideally, this room should have a window for him to look out of. Consider playing music on low volume and spend some time playing and cuddling with him each day. Make sure he has plenty of toys to amuse himself with.

You can't tone down Mother Nature and you usually can't stop progress, but you can take the necessary steps in your own home to make it feel feline friendly to Bruno.

## INDOORS IS BEST

Indoor cats live longer than their outdoor counterparts. Statistics from the Humane Society of the United States show that outdoor cats, on average, live to age five. Indoor cats, however, often live into their late teens, even early twenties.

While some outdoor cats do live long and healthy lives, they are exposed to many more dangers. Outdoor cats face increased risk of injury and illness. Many meet untimely ends under the wheels of cars or from animal attacks.

Learn more about making your feline a happy homebody by visiting the Indoor Cat Initiative Web site sponsored by Ohio State University's School of Veterinary Medicine.

## DECLAWING DISCUSSION

Declawing is an easy option for people who don't want their furniture or their skin scratched, but this is a very unpleasant procedure for cats. To put it bluntly, it would be like someone removing the tips of your fingers. Cats without claws can't experience the pleasure of scratching. They are vulnerable outdoors as they lose their protective weapons and can't climb trees to escape, so any declawed cat must live strictly indoors.

Years ago, declawing seemed to be part of a package deal. When a cat came in to be neutered or spayed, the option of declawing the front paws was offered. That's what happened to my cat Little Guy. Since I wanted an indoor cat, my veterinarian performed the procedure without much discussion. That was before I truly knew about the consequences of declawing.

In 2003, the American Veterinary Medical Association (AVMA) advised veterinarians to educate clients on alternatives to surgery and on the risks associated with any surgery. The Cat Fanciers' Association (CFA) disapproves of routine declawing because the procedure is unnecessary and provides no benefit to the cat. Some cat fanciers contend that declawing can have a negative impact on a cat's behavior, but this has not yet been proven by scientific research.

No one likes their furniture shredded, but no cat deserves to be relinquished to an animal shelter for doing what comes naturally and using his claws. Other options include clipping the front claws every two to four weeks, applying vinyl nail caps to your cat's nails, and providing scratching posts and other feline-welcoming furniture to scratch and claw.

In cases where there is high risk of injury to children, elderly persons with thin skin, those with bleeding disorders, or those vulnerable to disease transmission because of compromised immune systems, then declawing may be justified in order to maintain the cat-human bond. If all the alternatives have been tried without success, it is better for a cat to be in his home than relinquished to a shelter or abandoned.

Final note: Tendonectomy surgery, which is sometimes suggested as an alternative to declawing, is not recommended by the CFA or the AVMA.

# Scratching Solutions

**Q** I've accepted the fact that my cat needs to scratch. My problem is that I haven't had much luck in picking out the right scratching post for her. I tried a small bargain-priced scratching post, but she kept knocking it over. Then I lugged home a big cat tree from a garage sale, but she sniffs it and ignores it. I don't want to keep wasting money, but I don't want my furniture damaged either. Why is she so picky?

**A** This sounds like a feline version of *The Three Bears*. However, your cat is behaving quite normally. The reason she rejected the first post is because it was simply too tiny to accommodate her weight or her muscle. It would be like you trying to enjoy a meal at a restaurant sitting in a booster chair made for toddlers.

The issue with the second option is "kitty cooties." You thought you landed a deal by buying a used cat tree, but your cat quickly sniffed out the tree's former user. Cats often don't like to share with strangers. Your cat clearly communicated her disdain for the secondhand cat tree by avoiding it.

Before you invest in a third choice, spend some time watching your cat as she seeks out a scratching spot. Does she reach up high against the arm of the sofa or stretch out along the carpet? Use her habits to provide her with the most suitable option and provide her with some choices.

A horizontal surface should be large enough to accommodate both paws and sturdy enough to stay in place while being used. Many cats like the corrugated cardboard of this style of scratcher, which is not very expensive.

For a vertical post, make sure that the base is heavy and broad enough to handle your cat's weight and tugging. Scratching posts must be tall enough for your cat to stand on her hind legs and fully stretch her front paws. Look for one at least 32 inches high. If it wobbles or moves when you poke it, it won't stand up to use by an actual cat.

You also need to evaluate what material most appeals to your cat. Some cats prefer tactile textures, such as sisal (rope), bark, or wood. Other felines flock to knobby, loosely woven fabrics. Some like simple designs made of carpet or cardboard. Some cats can't resist scratching posts or trees that feature attached toys on springs or dangling ropes. Cater to your cat's preference when shopping.

Locate the scratching post or tree in a place your cat spends a lot of time. Make it more tempting by sprinkling some fresh catnip on it. Give her a couple of different options in different rooms.

As editor of *Catnip,* I supervise testing of products. Each month, a team of test cats (and kittens) and a contributing writer assess and evaluate a variety of products designed for felines. When we tested an assortment of scratching posts and trees, the winners were those that proved to be the most stable, those that fit snugly on the arms of sofas, and those that offered angles for both horizontal and vertical scratching.

Every cat deserves her own furniture for unsheathing her claws. So think like a cat when you shop. This is no time to shop on the cheap. In the end, you will save your sofa — and your sanity — by choosing a scratching post or tree that your cat will use for many years to come.

# Equipping a Cat

**Q** For years, my husband and I have owned dogs. We're nearing retirement and our beloved dog recently passed away. We both have some physical limitations and think we had better not have another dog, but we still want a pet to love. We have decided to adopt a cat. What should we do to prepare before we bring our new friend home?

**A** I salute you both for recognizing that a cat is better suited to your lifestyle as you enter your golden years. A cat does have different needs than a dog, though some items will be the same. For starters, your shopping cart needs to contain two litter boxes, clumping litter, a litter scoop, food bowl, water bowl, a breakaway collar, identification tag (with your phone number), brush and comb, nail clipper, appropriate food (depending on the age of the cat), treats, a sturdy scratching post, a comfy bed, a leash, harness, and, most important, toys!

Select toys that are safe. Avoid any with small pieces such as fake eyes that your cat might chew off and swallow. Better choices are toys that tap your kitten's predatory nature, such as feathers on wands, mouse mitts (fabric gloves with long, dangly fingers), and treat balls.

Scout each room of your house and be on the lookout for anything that could cause peril to your new feline. Specifically, make sure you don't leave dental floss, balls of yarn, sewing thread, or other string within reach. (Watch out for tinsel at Christmas!) These items can cause strangulation or can be ingested by a curious cat, possibly causing fatal internal injuries.

The initial investment may cause a bit of sticker shock, but once you have the essentials, your monthly budget should not be overly taxed by the presence of a cat. My final recommendation is that you consider purchasing pet health insurance. Even though your cat may be destined for a long and healthy life as an indoor cat, you can't predict when injury or illness may occur. Protect your cat — and your pocketbook — by obtaining pet insurance while your kitten is young and the premium is low.

# Wanted: A Room with a View

**Q** My cat, Chuckles, is quite the jokester. He loves to play and dash around the house. He also insists on trying to perch his big body on the narrow window ledge in the living room. He is always jumping up and falling off. There is a window ledge in my upstairs study that is wide enough for him to sit on, but when I put him on it, he jumps down. Why does he insist on trying to sit on a ledge that is clearly too narrow for him?

**A** Chuckles knows where he can view the best action of outdoor activities in your neighborhood. Cats are nosey neighbors. They love to spend hours eyeing what's happening in your yard and at the next-door neighbor's house. Chuckles is clearly telling you that he wants to check out what's going on outside your living room window. He can probably see more birds, squirrels, or other critters from there than from your upstairs window.

The easy solution — and one that can still blend into your home décor — is to install a window ledge that can handle his wide girth. Don't worry. You won't have to do any drilling or poke any holes in your drywall. Many sturdy, stylish window ledges fasten securely with suction cups and sticky strips. They also feature plush or fleece-lined covers that come in a variety of colors and can be easily machine washed.

If you don't want to add a cat perch to your windowsill, consider placing a cat post with a platform next to this favored spot so that Chuckles can sit in comfort. Another solution might be a dining room chair, with a towel to protect the upholstery, which can easily be removed when you have company and put back in time for the next day's viewing.

Treat Chuckles to a comfortable seat in the living room where he can occupy a lot of his home-alone time scouting the neighborhood, and he'll be less apt to perform any unwanted behaviors. While you're at home, he may even meow you over to catch a glimpse of a rare bird or to check out the funny socks that your neighbor is sporting.

# Dashing Out the Door

**Q** Whenever I leave or enter the house through the door leading to the garage, my big orange tabby, Morris, stands ready to bolt out the door. He is quite a muscular, pushy cat. Sometimes I can't reach the garage door opener quickly enough to shut the overhead garage door before Morris scoots out and down the driveway. He's supposed to be an indoor cat, so I have to run after him and bring him home, which can take a long time. What can I do to keep Morris from bolting out the door?

**A** What makes an indoor cat feel the need to prowl outside? Morris may be smelling and hearing other cats, especially during the breeding seasons, or he may be curious about the trees and grass he can see from the window (not to mention the birds!). He obviously hates to be a homebody. He doesn't understand that he is safer inside. He also thinks he can throw his weight around with you.

You can retrain Morris to meet and greet you at a particular spot when you leave or return home. Practice luring Morris over to a favorite place, such as a window perch or a cat tree. Then say your good-byes there. Give him a special treat or a pinch of catnip to occupy him while you exit. If he likes to chase things, take a paper wad, crinkle it in your hand to make enticing sounds, and toss it in the opposite direction as you exit. Or toss him a toy mouse to distract him. Also, randomly choose different doors to enter and leave. A cat can't lay in wait at three different exits. Practice with the main garage door shut, so that even if Morris turns into Houdini, you'll be able to recapture him easily.

When you come home, close the garage door while you practice your returns. Walk in the house door, completely ignoring the ever-waiting Morris. Go over to the chosen spot. Call him over, greet him, and offer him a treat. The idea is to motivate Morris to move away from the door when you leave and when you come home in exchange for a tasty payoff at the window perch or cat tree.

Another method is to discourage him from approaching the door at all. One of my friends had a similar problem with her bolting cat. She placed squirt guns on either side of the exit door. When she was coming or going, she aimed low and squirted her cat in the chest area. It caught him off guard enough to cause him not to stand so close to the door any more. Just take careful aim and do not splash Morris in the face. A noisy shaker (you can make one from an empty soda can with a few pennies taped inside) or a few sharp claps of your hand might chase him away long enough for you to get through the door safely.

Consider satisfying your cat's need to experience the outdoors by installing a window enclosure or taking him for walks. Fit him in a harness attached to a leash and let him sniff and scout out what's happening on your block. Many cats can become accustomed to wearing a leash if you take it slowly and reward them for small steps. (See Walk This Way, page 293, for more on leash training.)

If Morris does escape, please don't scold him or reprimand him when he returns to the house. You will only confuse him and possibly dampen his desire to come home.

# In Search of "Fang" Shui

**Q** I want to tinker with my interior a bit to better accommodate my four indoor cats, who range in age from two to ten. They all get along, but I suspect they are a bit bored when I'm at work during the day. They sleep a lot and need to exercise more. However, I do not want to spend a lot of money or turn my house into, well, a cathouse! I don't want to be labeled a crazy cat lady. I also don't want to turn it into a place that I can't sell sometime in the future. Any tips on cat design projects?

**A** Your quartet is quite fortunate to have you in their lives. Don't worry, you are anything but a crazy cat lady. In fact, you represent two other *C* words: caring and considerate. You can renovate your place to make it more feline appealing without turning it into a place that would have limited appeal to future buyers.

**FELINE FACT**

A group of kittens is called a "kindle" and a group of adult cats is called a "clowder."

If you're handy with a drill and hammer, you can install a sturdy shelf in a corner for your cats to perch from on high, instead of changing the entire look of the room with a catwalk that runs the entire length of a wall. You can lean a sisal-covered plank up to a bookcase nook or partially wrap a floor to ceiling post in the den or rec room with sisal for your cats so they can act like feline firefighters, scaling up and down the pole.

Even if you're reluctant to drill holes in your walls, you can make your place look like a fashion showcase while catering to your cat's needs. Among the new products available for felines and their décor-conscious owners are big, soft pillows, cat condos that match your furniture, designer feeders and water bowls, and litter boxes disguised as houseplant containers.

Finally, you can make use of certain features in your home to hide cat necessities, such as litter boxes. Alice Moon-Fanelli shares an interior design solution she offered to a client whose cat was urinating outside the litter box, including in the fireplace. The client did not want to put a litter box in the living room. Upon further questioning, Dr. Moon-Fanelli learned that the fireplace was not in working order and was never used. So, she suggested that the client place a litter box in the fireplace and cover the opening with a decorative fireplace screen. The cat's needs were met and no more incidents of inappropriate urination were reported.

This is a start for you to unleash your imagination, not open your pocketbook. You can probably come up with other creative ways to make your interior more feline-friendly to your fabulous foursome.

# Abyssinian Introductions

**EDNA AND AL HAD EAGERLY AWAITED** the arrival of Ruffian, a 16-week-old Abyssinian kitten. Her breeders shipped progress photos, special litter, food treats, and a care manual for this kitten about to join a two-cat household. Knowing acceptance by resident cats might be complicated, I provided a multistep introduction plan.

Edna's special "prince" was an eight-year-old, neutered Abyssinian male with an only-cat, one-person attitude, and a high energy level. The "grande dame," at 19 years old, was quite frail and showing signs of senility. She preferred a quiet lap-sitting existence and well-established routine. Both were more bonded to their owners than to each other.

A well-socialized, four-month-old Aby is usually self-confident and will enthusiastically meet new cats and human friends. Adult resident cats, however, do not initially welcome a newcomer. Similar to their cousins in the wild, domestic cats display protective territorial traits that require gradual exposure during introductions.

Even after a long flight and car ride, Ruffian arrived at her new home with play on her mind. A bathroom was prepared with a comfortable cozy blanket, toys, litter, and food, but when Ruffy jumped up on the counter, she was shocked to see another kitten in the mirror. Step One in my introduction instructions — providing a "safe room" — suddenly turned into a catastrophe. A shaking and terrified kitten watched the mirror being covered with newspaper pages to block the view.

Once Ruffy had calmed down, we were ready for the second step of exchanging smells over a few days. This involved allowing the resident cats to sniff Ruffy's carrier and blanket in the safe room, while the kitten became acquainted with the rest of the house.

Step Three called for the first glimpse between the resident cats and the kitten through a glass door. There was some hissing, but Ruffy was thrilled to finally see another Abyssinian. She happily ran around, launching herself onto the kitchen counter and eventually crashing into the other cats' water dishes. From then on, it was clear she was no longer satisfied with life in the safe room.

Then came the final step — contact. The resident cats were held so they could sniff and greet Ruffy, who was also restrained. The senior female cat acted uninterested but expressed her protest by retreating. The male appeared miffed but politely avoided lashing out. Finally, with mealtime as a distraction, all three began to mingle peacefully.

Today, the three cats may not be best buds, but harmony exists. As for Ruffy, she displays a typical Aby personality by enjoying a ride on top of the vacuum.

*Contributed by Joan Miller, all-breed judge*

# **Bring the Outdoors In**

**Q** My cat is driving me crazy! I adopted him from the local shelter a couple of months ago. He is about a year old. I want him to be an indoor cat, but he is constantly demanding to go outside. I have to be very careful when I open my door or he will try to slip out. I own a home with a backyard, but I can't afford to fence the whole thing in. I tried to train him to walk on a leash, but that was a disaster. Are there other ways I can safely satisfy his need to be outdoors?

**A** Clearly, your kitty craves the sights, sounds, and smells of the outdoors. It is likely that he was an outside cat before you adopted him, but if you are patient, you can probably persuade him to adapt to indoor life. You don't want his demands or door bolting to escalate into deeper behavior problems. His indoor-only status can cause more stress and anxiety, so you need to provide distractions for him.

Many creative companies are designing a variety of outdoor enclosures that give cats the outdoors minus the dangers. They vary in size and price, ranging from window enclosures to freestanding gazebo-type enclosures positioned in the backyard. Some are freestanding while others are attached to the house and accessed through a cat flap door. All of these enclosures are designed to keep your cat safe while allowing him some time outside.

Some of these models can take a major bite out of your household budget, but might be worth the cost if your cat is calmer and happier when he has an outlet for his outdoor longing. Even something as simple as a window enclosure will give your cat the chance to soak up vitamin D from the sun and be out of paw's reach from dangerous predators such as dogs or coyotes.

> **FELINE FACT**
> Sir Isaac Newton, discoverer of the principles of gravity, also invented the cat door.

The more elaborate outdoor enclosures include screened-in designs that can fill a good portion of your backyard. Inside one of these, your cat can play on the grass, climb a tree, and chase bugs safely. You can also place ready-made cat posts and trees inside the enclosure for your cat to claw and climb and cuddle inside cubbyholes.

Please keep safety in mind for whatever enclosure you choose. Make sure that it is attached to your home or within easy sight. The enclosure should offer both sunny and shady spots, contain fresh water, and meet any zoning laws of your municipality.

# Power of Play

**Q** My two dogs enjoy playing together and with us. But my cat, Mandy, is content to just watch. Once they grow out of kittenhood, do cats really want to play? Do they need to play? Mandy seems happy grooming herself, sitting on my lap, eating, and sleeping. Should I be concerned?

**A** Adult cats are not hairy, dust-collecting pieces of furniture. Like their canine counterparts, felines do want — and need — to play. All grooming, napping, and eating can make Mandy a dull cat. I am a big promoter of play with a purpose. Teaching your cat to play effectively can improve her social skills and her level of fitness. Play helps keep feline hearts healthy, joints limber, and muscles strong. It also allows cats to practice hunting and play-fighting skills and strengthens their connection with you. Keeping your cat active will prevent her from becoming obese. And regular exercise will keep her mentally alert as well.

Kittens learn how to behave like cats through playtime supervised by their moms. The basis of play for cats falls into two areas: social and object-oriented. Social play involves other

**FELINE FACT**

The record for killing the most mice by a feline belongs to Towser, a Scottish tabby who killed 28,899 mice over the span of 21 years. That's an average of about four mice per day. Towser died in 1987.

cats, family pets — like your two dogs — and people. Object play involves manipulating a toy or other item that hones a cat's dexterity.

Although some cats are born to play, Mandy appears to need a little encouragement. One way to motivate her is with the right toy. My brother, Kevin, has a toy chest filled with a variety of feline items for his cat, Lager. They include a ping-pong ball, catnip mice on strings, and wads of paper and foil. Like many play-minded cats, Lager will initiate games by rubbing against Kevin's legs and then dashing away. Other play cues include pawing at your arm and delivering steady eye-to-eye stares.

Enlist the aid of one of your cat-friendly dogs. Try tying a long string on to your dog's collar. As your dog walks around the house, he'll drag the string along the floor. That should bring out Mandy's pouncing proclivities. Remember, with cats, it is all about movement. They like to hunt, stalk, and chase objects that are mobile. Just make sure that the dog is in a playful mood and up for the cat's antics. For safety reasons, always supervise closely and end the game on a happy note.

Please be persistent and encouraging. It may take some time for Mandy to turn into a playful cat. Be sure to praise her and whoop it up so she knows this is a special time with you. Once Mandy views you as the Queen of Feline Play and comes to feel that she is as valued a pal as your two dogs are, you may discover a wonderful new side to her personality.

## MASTERS OF FELINE DESIGN

My friends Bob Walker and Frances Mooney share
their San Diego home with a dozen rescue cats.
Despite the crowd, these kitties don't have tiffs or
urine-mark in the house, because Bob and Frances
have created a feline fantasyland. This talented,
cat-happy couple used inexpensive materials to
create a jungle gym that satisfies the most curious
of cats.

There are cats everywhere, thanks to floor-to-
ceiling scratching poles, catwalks, ramps, and cubby-

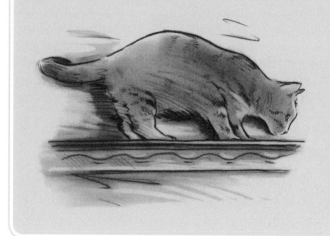

holes. Four hundred feet of sisal is wrapped around a column and a ceiling-high ledge, where the cats snooze contentedly. An "elevated highway" made of painted plywood crisscrosses the rooms. There are even holes cut in the walls to provide passage between rooms. Brightly colored paint and fun details add to the unique look.

In their book, *The Cats' House,* Bob and Frances share tips on how to build ramps, catwalks, and other feline features. Each year they open their home for touring, with proceeds donated to a local cat protection society.

In this house, there are no worries about a sofa being clawed or a sock being stolen. There are far too many cat-cool functional furnishings to occupy the minds and physical needs of the tabby troop. As Bob puts it, "If possession is nine-tenths of the law, then our place is truly the cats' house. After all, our cats are at home more than we are."

# The Joy of Toys

**Q** My five-year-old cat, Indie, has so much energy that he tires me out. He is constantly bugging me to play with him, even though I give him plenty of attention. Can you suggest some safe toys that will keep him busy and allow me to be able to read a book without his persistent pawing?

**A** Are you sure you don't have a Labrador puppy disguised as a cat? It brings a smile to my face to hear of felines who love to play well into their adult years. But I can empathize with your request to be able to read a book, watch a television show, or work on the computer without Indie's persistent pleading.

Indie seems to have a giant need to exercise. Since cats aren't welcome at the local gyms to work up a sweat and unleash their pent-up energies, you need to bring the gym to your cat. I'm not talking about bringing in live mice for Indie to hunt or planting a tree in the middle of your living room for him to climb, though he would probably enjoy both of those! But do provide him with a couple of places that he can jump up onto — perhaps a carpeted cat tree with several levels or a shelf in a corner overlooking the television room.

Another suggestion is to encourage Indie to play with his food. Instead of filling his bowl with kibble, make mealtime a tasty treasure hunt. Scoop up pieces of kibble and place them on each step of a stair or on a long hallway for Indie to sniff out and eat. Do this each morning before you leave for work to occupy his time and again in the early evening when you come home and want to relax. You can also put some special treats in a treat ball that features small openings. When nudged or pawed, the ball moves and releases tasty prizes one at a time. Watch Indie as he goes on a food hunt.

**FELINE FACT**

Don't let an urban legend cloud the truth. Veterinary toxicologists report that Febreze fabric freshener products are safe for use in households with cats as long as you follow label instructions for use.

As editor of *Catnip* magazine, I enjoy the opportunity to test products, including toys, for our feline friends. Here are some types of products that have been tested and given paws up approval by the team of *Catnip* test cats.

**BALLS IN BOXES.** These toys resemble the feline version of a Rubik's cube. Some of the more popular ones feature square-shaped pressboard boxes with holes on the top and sides that are big enough to insert toy balls for cats to fish out with their paws.

**ROUND AND ROUND WE GO.** For cats who love to give chase, try a ball in a heavy plastic track that goes round and round with each paw swat. In the center of some track balls are corrugated cardboard insert pads suitable for scratching. Cats get the double bonus of stalking a ball and honing their claws.

**MOVING TOYS.** Toys with batteries and a remote control device rotate and move erratically to mimic insect motion. Some of these toys come in the shape of popular cat cartoon characters like Garfield.

My final advice: Please book 10 to 15 minutes of interactive playtime each day with Indie as well. Teach Indie some tricks through clicker training or introduce him to indoor agility. (See Click! Click! Train Your Tabby, page 280, and Make Way for Feline Athletes, page 284.) You are doing your part to build his confidence and keep him in shape. As invaluable as keep-busy toys are, they should never be used as replacements for that special bonding time you can share with your playful pup, er, I mean puss!

---

### TOYS ON THE NO-NO LIST

Don't let your cat play with the following items. They are too easily swallowed or wrapped around a neck.

- Yarn
- Dental floss
- Rubber bands
- Paper clips
- Plastic bags
- Dangling curtain cords

---

# Shadow Walking

**Q** All four of my cats will follow my dog and me on our walks, but most of them give up after a block or so. Riley, however, is very persistent and will follow us no matter how far we go. She yowls and meows until I stop and wait for her to catch up. Usually, we keep our walks short when we get "caught" by Riley, but one time, she followed us all the way around a nearby tennis court. She crossed streets and walked through several open areas to keep up. Why does she follow me if it seems so stressful?

**A** This is a case of kitty see, kitty go. Clearly, Riley is a very confident cat who trusts you, your dog, your surroundings, and herself. Cats do not typically walk in open areas if they sense any danger. They are more apt to hide in shrubbery and scout out the nearest tree limbs in case of danger.

But not Ms. Riley. Chalk this habit up to her powerful personality. I would not take her vocalizing as stress as much as it is her wish to be chatty on your outings. Talk back to her in an upbeat tone. She just wants to be part of the pack. You should take this as a big feline compliment.

My cat Corky would follow anyone carrying a fishing pole because he associated the pole with a tasty bluegill meal. I even experimented a few times by walking out the front door with the fishing pole but moving in the opposite direction from our backyard lake. Corky happily trotted by my side anyway. Perhaps he thought I was merely taking the scenic route to the fish-filled lake.

**FELINE FACT**
Most cats have no eyelashes.

It sounds like your neighborhood is quiet and without a lot of traffic, and that you keep tabs on your feline entourage, especially the roaming Riley. Still, I recommend that you train Riley to use a made-for-cats harness so that you can reel her in should any sudden danger surface. And it's a good idea to do a head count to make sure all the cats are inside before you and the dog head out for a long walk or run.

## FELINE WILL POWER

What happens if you die before your cat? Or become ill or incapacitated? Do you have a plan for her care? Including your cat in your will or living trust is one of the best gifts you can give your feline friend. I recommend that you work with an attorney who specializes in estate planning to draw up a will or trust that officially expresses your intentions for your cat's care.

Wills and trusts are often read weeks or months after someone dies. That's why it is also important to name a couple of caregivers who have agreed to step in and assist your cat as soon as something happens to you. Spell out your wishes in writing by carrying a wallet "alert card" and letting your friends and family know what your arrangements are.

Making contingency plans like these is not a fun task, but once completed, you will have peace of mind in knowing that your pets will be taken care of after your passing. See resources, page 314 for more information.

# Click! Click! Train Your Tabby

**Q** My husband and I have different views on whether cats are capable of learning tricks. My husband believes that cats are out to please only themselves and have no interest in doing some of the tricks that dogs do willingly. I believe that with the right motivation, we can train our cat to shake paws, sit up, and other commands. I hope you can settle this bet. Which one of us is right?

**A** You win this bet, paws down. Cats are not commonly thought of as performers, but many do participate in circuses, street shows, and movies. One effective method for working with cats is clicker training. Clicker training involves the use a distinctive sound to reinforce desired actions. Karen Pryor, a world-renowned animal behaviorist, first used clicker training on dolphins. A couple of decades ago, she began employing her clicker training on dogs, cats, and other critters. She is regarded as the pioneer in this training technique for pets.

Clicker training is a positive technique that relies on operant conditioning to shape a desired action or behavior without force or cajoling. The premise is simple: encourage the animal to perform desired actions by rewarding appropriate behavior. Clicker training works because there is no punishment involved. You draw attention to the behaviors you're seeking in your cat and ignore other actions.

As for your own cat, here are some ways you can bring out his true talents through clicker training. You can buy a small, plastic clicker at most pet supply stores, or you can use a ballpoint pen. Whichever you use, it is important that you stick with it so that its distinctive sound serves as a cue for your feline student. Make the clicking sound and then offer a small treat. In the first few sessions, you are merely introducing the clicker sound to your cat and establishing that the sound equals a treat.

Timing is key to clicker training's success. When your cat does something you want, for example raising his front paw, you need to press the clicker, hand over a small treat, and immediately say "paw" to reinforce the desired behavior. In time, the light bulb will turn on inside your cat's head as he starts to recognize the link between the word "paw" and the sound of the reinforcing click.

To use a clicker to teach your cat to sit on cue, start by luring him into a sitting position with a food treat or target stick that you slowly move over his head toward his back. Let gravity be your ally. As his head follows the treat, his back end will naturally touch the floor. When this happens, click and hand over the treat. Clicking signals "mission accomplished." If he

doesn't sit, do nothing. Do not give a treat or say a word. Let him figure out what provides him with a tasty dividend and what doesn't.

You need only invest a few minutes each day in clicker-training sessions with your cat. Felines learn best in mini-sessions, not marathon lectures. Their attention spans tend to evaporate after five or ten minutes. Conduct your training sessions in a quiet place where you can work without distractions. Time the training before a meal, so that your hungry cat will be more motivated to learn.

Using a clicker, you can train your cat to perform a few basic commands as well as other things limited only by your imagination and your cat's preferences. You can teach your cat to do the cha-cha, for example, if he likes to walk forward and backward when he follows you into the kitchen. You can also train your cat to move in a circle, shake with his front paw, or even meow on cue.

The beauty of clicker training comes in the payoff. You end up with a more mentally stimulated cat and a stronger friendship bond with him. Once your cat is consistently completing some clicker-trained tricks, stage a performance for your husband and watch his amazement at these feline feats.

(See Strays Turned Stars, page 160, for more on performing cats and Master of the Ring, page 302, for information about cat agility.)

## TOP 10 RULES FOR TRAINING CATS

1. Always say your cat's name to get his attention before giving any command.

2. Be consistent with your verbal and hand signals.

3. Pay attention to your cat's mood. Train him when he is receptive to learning, not when the lessons fit your schedule.

4. Select a quiet time and room where you can be one-on-one with your cat.

5. Be positive, patient, and encouraging.

6. Provide small food rewards and enthusiastic praise immediately after each success, no matter how small.

7. Start with the basic commands of *come, sit,* and *stay.*

8. Break the desired behavior into smaller steps and build on each one.

9. Teach your cat only one new trick or behavior at a time. Cats are not multitasking masters.

10. Keep training sessions simple and short — no more than five to ten minutes at a time.

# Make Way for Feline Athletes

**Q** For the past few years, I have enjoyed competing in agility with my Australian shepherd. It is good exercise and a lot of fun for both of us. Recently, I adopted a very smart Siamese cat through a breed rescue group. Simone is two years old. We bonded very quickly. She follows me around the house like a dog, chats to me, and likes to learn. She sits and shakes paws on command. I've read about agility for cats. Can you offer me more insight?

**A** Move over, Rover! Dogs don't have a monopoly when it comes to demonstrating their athletic abilities in public. Agility is all about running an obstacle course in a timely fashion. This relatively young sport is starting to catch on across North America, especially among athletic cats with outgoing personalities. In general, Siamese cats do quite well in agility because of their intelligence and, dare we say, dog-like nature when it comes to learning.

Feline agility consists of a timed obstacle course. Cats compete one at a time in runs that include carpeted steps, weave poles, hoop jumps, tunnels, and hurdles of various heights. Some competitions also include ladders, tables, and ramps. Handlers motivate the cats by having them follow a lure or target through an obstacle course.

As you know from your canine competitions, accuracy is more crucial than speed. Competitors earn points for successfully conquering obstacles in a prescribed order. Your chances for winning decrease if your cat does not perform an obstacle or takes them out of order.

Some cats may be great agility athletes but prefer to be homebodies. If that describes Simone, you can create an indoor agility course for her by using household furnishings that include dining room chairs, tabletops, ottomans, and sturdy plastic boxes with lids. Be imaginative — you can use a hula hoop to act as a tire ring jump for your cat to leap through. Whether you travel to public competitions or just play in the privacy of your home, agility provides your cat with great exercise and a great chance to show off. Let the fun and games begin! (See Masters of the Ring, page 302, for more on agility.)

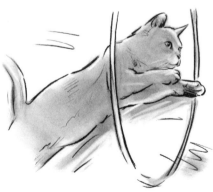

# One and Only

**Q** We love our cat, Polly. We named her that because she often perches on my husband's shoulder like a parrot. A lot of our friends have two or more cats. Some remark that Polly has to be lonely being the only cat in the household. We think she is just fine. How can we tell if she is lonely or if she likes being an only pet?

**A** Please don't be pressured by your well-intentioned friends to add another pet to your home. There's nothing wrong with having a single cat. A lot of people enjoy having only one pet to lavish with attention and affection. The trick is finding the right cat and knowing the signs that indicate he or she is quite content without a feline pal.

My friend Debb has a two-year-old Siamese named Kri who rules the roost. Debb works long hours, but when she puts the key in her front door, Kri is there waiting with his favorite plush toy, Mr. Lion, in his mouth. Debb immediately greets Kri and plays with him for a few minutes before even taking off her coat.

When Debb travels, she arranges for Kri to stay at a friend's house. This cat's world revolves around one person and that is just perfectly fine with him. He doesn't need or want feline companionship because he receives plenty of love and attention from Debb.

Some cats are better off being the one and only in the house. Likely contenders for single-cat status include older cats, those with sensitive health issues, those who are FIV-positive, those who are territorial, and those who are very shy or nervous. Cats who have been raised with littermates or who have lived happily with other cats are more likely to enjoy having a feline housemate.

Unlike dogs, solo cats rarely, if ever, display the classic signs of separation anxiety. You won't find your home-alone cat clawing the front door or digging up the carpet — common behaviors exhibited by anxious canines. There are ways, however, that a cat who is overly attached to a person might demonstrate how they miss that person when he or she is away. These behaviors include grooming excessively, vocalizing, or urinating outside the litter box.

Just because Polly is your one and only pet doesn't mean she has to be lonely or bored. Make sure you play with her each day and talk with her. Keep her indoor life enriched and exciting by swapping out her cat toys. You can provide Polly with puzzle or track toys, play animal videos on your television, and offer her climbing trees and/or an enclosed outdoor observation area. Two favorite ideas of mine are positioning a bird feeder outside within full view of a window your cat can see out of and adding a fish tank to your house. Just be kind to those fish by making sure the aquarium is fitted with a cat-proof lid.

Medically and emotionally, there are some pluses to having a one-cat household. You are able to spot health problems sooner. You tend to notice changes in your cat's eating or litter box habits more quickly than your friends who have two or more cats. Noticing early warning signs can increase your chances for successful diagnosis and treatment.

# Poof! Disappearing Cat!

**Q** Recently, my neighbor's Japanese Bobtail became lost when a repairman left the back door open. We organized a neighborhood search for Jinx, and fortunately, we found him the next day hiding in shrubbery about three houses away. As an owner of two indoor cats, I worry about what would happen if they should suddenly find themselves outside. Why would contented indoor cats want to venture outside on their own? What tips can you offer for doing a thorough job of looking for them?

**A** You're in good company. All of us with indoor cats feel a bit nervous when we think about the possibility of our pampered pets facing the dangers of the outside world. As a young adult, I had a cat named Samantha who loved to hang out in my front yard with a lightweight chain attached to her collar. I always supervised her, but one time I dashed inside to answer the phone and when I came out five minutes later, she was gone! All that remained was her collar still attached to the chain. I called and searched for days but didn't spot her for nearly two months, when she appeared on my neighbor's porch. She needed veterinary care because she was dehydrated, but she survived and I felt fortunate to have her back.

Even contented feline homebodies possess natural hunting instincts and curiosity. The sights, sounds, and smells of the outdoors can prove to be far more alluring than simply sunning on the sofa. Cats think in the present. A door opens and the cat slips out. He doesn't make contingency plans for what happens if forgets his way home. But we can better the chances of finding our cats if we recognize typical lost-cat behaviors.

Most indoor cats who slip out a door do not venture very far. Indoor cats tend to hide rather than flee because hiding is an instinctive response. That said, they can be darn good at hiding and extremely challenging to coax out of hard-to-reach spots.

Know your cat's personality. That's important because it will aid in finding him. You may be interested to learn that cats fall into four general personality types. Let me share with you the best game plan for finding each of these types.

**XENOPHOBIC CATS** are scared of anything new or the unknown. They tend to dash and hide when guests come into your home and refuse to resurface until hours after the guests depart. If they find themselves outside, these cats tend to freeze out of fear and do not go far. If you have such a cat who gets lost, the best plan is to set a baited humane trap near your home. Place a dish of tuna inside to lure your cat into the trap.

**CAUTIOUS CATS** initially disappear when guests come to your home, but then slowly enter the room to check out the newcomers. If your cat fits this description, then conduct a thorough search of surrounding homes and set baited humane traps in your neighbors' yards. These cats, once they muster the courage, tend to come out of hiding after a day or so and try to retrace their steps back home. They may even meow while hiding if they hear your voice.

**ALOOF CATS** will avoid people they don't know, including members of a search-and-rescue group. This type will eventually come out of hiding and either show up meowing at your door or start to travel. For these cats, the best plan is to set up baited humane traps throughout the neighborhood, while searching yards and other areas near where they escaped.

**OUTGOING, CURIOUS CATS** act like the ambassador to your home. They enjoy meeting and greeting your guests. If you have a cat that matches this description, be aware that he is likely to wander as he is not easily frightened. The best game plan with this type involves speaking with neighbors, because your cat may have charmed one of them into bringing him inside and feeding him.

When searching for your cat, resist running, because swift movement might frighten him and cause him to go into deeper hiding. Don't simply ask neighbors to look around for your cat. Instead, ask if you can nose around under their decks and other hiding places. Your cat is more likely to come to you than to a stranger.

If you happen to have more than one indoor cat and they get along very well, consider putting the feline pal inside a carrier and taking her with you when you search the area. The scent of this cat may be enough to lure your lost cat out of hiding.

For any indoor cat who becomes lost, post brightly colored posters within a radius of several blocks. Make the posters eye-catching and include a photo of your cat, his name, your contact info, and perhaps a reward. And don't forget other avenues such as contacting area veterinary clinics, local shelters, animal control, and police departments in your locale.

> **FELINE FACT**
>
> In 1952, a Texas tabby named Dusty set the record for prodigious progeny by having more than 420 kittens. She had her last litter at the age of 18.

Let me offer one final strategy: if possible, leave a sliding door open four to six inches or a back door or garage door propped open a bit. Some cats wait until dark to come out of hiding and may come back home when they feel it is safe to do so. You may be relieved in the morning at the sight of your "lost" cat sitting next to her bowl waiting for breakfast.

# Let's See Some ID

**Q** My indoor cat, Chance, wears an identification tag on his collar. He never seems to want to go outside. My beagle, on the other hand, doesn't always come when he is called. I spent the money on a microchip ID for the dog, but I don't see the need to do the same for Chance. Am I wrong?

**A** Even though Chance loves the indoor life, he could find himself lost. We can't control our cats' movements every moment. He may become lost during a car trip, if a door is left open in your home, or under other circumstances.

The cost of microchipping is quite affordable these days and is totally priceless when it comes to reuniting lost pets with their grateful owners. Contact your veterinarian or local animal shelter to find out more about the procedure. Many clinics and shelters offer discount microchipping on certain days of the month or during special events.

Even though Chance sports an identification tag, he could lose his collar. That's why I'm a big promoter of having pets microchipped. Microchipping does not automatically guarantee the safe return of your lost cat, but it sure increases the odds.

Microchipping is a quick and virtually painless procedure. Your cat does not need to be anesthetized. A veterinarian uses a special needle to insert the microchip (about the size of a grain of rice) under your cat's skin between the shoulder blades. A cat found with no outward signs of identification can be scanned for the presence of a microchip using a special wand device commonly found in animal shelters and veterinary clinics. The microchip provides your contact information as well as your veterinary clinic and the manufacturer of the chip.

Sadly, about 40 percent of people who microchip their pets fail to take the final processing step. The chip is useless if it does not contain your contact info. Make sure you fill out the enrollment paperwork and mail it in (with a nominal one-time fee) to the manufacturer of the chip or a national recovery service. Enrollment should be kept updated if you move, and having a recovery service that is available 24 hours/7 days is the best protection.

---

# Walk This Way

**Q** My cat, Sissy, is quite curious and very mellow. I just moved into a nice, quiet neighborhood after living in an apartment with her for a couple years. I would like to take her for walks to give her a chance to be outside. I don't want to risk losing her, so I want to teach her to walk on a leash. How can I go about this? Will she tolerate being on a leash?

**A** Your success in training your cat to walk on a leash outside depends first on your attitude. Trust me, cats can see through our bluffs. If you're apprehensive or unsure about the process or become impatient, your cat will read the message loud and clear.

Second, heed this cardinal cat rule: When it comes to sauntering outside on a tether, cats call the shots. Don't expect Sissy to start heeling like a poodle who just graduated top in her obedience training class. Sissy leads and you follow.

Third, a leash alone won't do the trick. You need to fit Sissy with a harness so there is no chance that she could become spooked and slip out of a collar and get lost. Do not use a small dog harness. You need one designed for cats so there is no chance for her to squirm out. The best are the figure-eight designs and walking jackets.

Harness training is best accomplished in the following stages:

1. When you bring home the harness and leash, leave them next to Sissy's food bowl or scratching post for a few days. Say nothing. Let her approach on her own to check them out.

2. When Sissy is in a relaxed, contented mood, engage her in a little play with the harness and leash. Dangle the harness and let her swat at it. Drag the leash on the floor to entice her to chase and pounce on it. You are associating these training tools with fun and games in your cat's mind.

3. Next, put the harness on Sissy inside your house and offer lots of praise and a couple of treats. Let her walk around freely wearing it. If she struggles or tries to rub the harness off, calmly remove it and repeat Step Two before trying again. But if she seems okay, let her wear the harness for a few minutes and then take it off.

4. It's time to attach the leash to your harness-wearing cat. Again, keep this stage indoors and monitor Sissy's level of acceptance. Not all cats are fans of harnesses, and you have to respect their personal preferences.

5. Once she has accepted walking around the house wearing a harness, you're ready to head outdoors. Limit your first outing to a safe haven such as your backyard or front porch. Remember, the goal is to build slowly on each success.

6. After a few days, you should be ready to head down your driveway and possibly a bit down the sidewalk. Pick quiet times in your neighborhood to limit possible distractions.

You want to make this a pleasant experience. Unless you have that rare cat who is eager to go for a long walk, keep your excursions short. If you live on a busy street, put your cat in a cat stroller and head for a quiet place like a park where she may feel more secure.

My cat Murphy is a proud harness-wearing, leash-walking feline. I think she gets a bit jealous when she sees me grab the leashes for my two dogs. But when I return, I often bring out her harness and leash and say, "Wanna go outside?" She races me to the front door. With the dogs, it is all about distance, but Murphy prefers a stroll with stops to smell flowers, flop and roll on the sun-kissed sidewalk, and nibble on a few blades of grass. We may not go far, but our brief jaunts prove to be filled with plenty of adventure for Murphy.

---

# Help for My Clinic-Hating Cat

**Q** I absolutely dread having to take my cat for his regular veterinary visits. Even when I don't do anything out of the ordinary, Oscar seems to sense when I am about to take him to the vet clinic and he hides under the bed. He often scratches me as I fight to pull him out. He howls all the way to the clinic and once there, he turns into Evil Kitty. It is quite difficult for my veterinarian to examine him. Oscar is a very healthy cat who lives inside. Can I just skip these visits? It seems more like torture than help.

**A** Most cats are not fans of the three C's: Car, Carrier, and Clinic. Oscar definitely does not put any of these on his Top 10 List of Feline Favorites. Even though you think you are not doing anything to tip him off, Oscar is tapping into changes in your body chemicals (you are more anxious) and body language (your muscles are more tense). That's all he needs to initiate the under-the-bed dash.

Some cats do well when they are cared for by veterinarians with feline-only practices, because there are none of those dreaded d-o-g-s hanging out in the lobby. But cats like Oscar would fare even better if they could

> **FELINE FACT**
> Cats have 290 bones in their bodies, compared to 206 bones in a human.

be seen in their homes. By examining frightened, fearfully aggressive, and people-phobic cats on their own turf, visiting veterinarians are able to obtain more accurate health readings on their patients. For example, some cats display artificially elevated blood glucose levels and blood pressure values due to stress when examined at a clinic. House-call vets can also gather clues about a cat's environment that may help in treating medical conditions. They get to see where the litter boxes are located and witness the interactions of the cat with other family pets.

House-call vets make sense for people who have three or more cats; forget about trying to bring that many cats all at once to the clinic. You are risking the chance of one escaping or your sanity being tested far more than it deserves. This way, you receive one-stop care instead of having to book multiple appointments.

Visiting vets are also the answer for people with busy schedules who have difficulty squeezing their cat's appointment in between their children's soccer and band practices; for people who can't drive; for those who may have medical conditions of their own; and for celebrities who prefer not to be mobbed by autograph hounds at a veterinary clinic.

House-call fees are not as steep as you may imagine, but prices do vary by location. So save your arm from scratches and keep Oscar's stress level from escalating by booking an appointment with a house-call vet. Check your local yellow pages for listings or look on the Internet.

---

# Yikes! We're Moving!

 I am moving to a new apartment in six months with Misha, my 11-year-old cat. I am wondering what I should be doing to make this move less stressful for her. She has had a history of urinary tract problems — all resolved — and with that came a habit of over-grooming to the point of pulling out her hair. She is alone all day, but I do play with her at night. I would refer to her as a bit high-strung. Any advice on how to make this move go smoothly for her?

**A** Moving is stressful for everyone. Cats detest breaks in their routines. The sight of furniture being moved, items being packed, and strange men coming in and out of their feline "castle" can take a toll on their self-confidence and trigger some unwanted behaviors (like hiding, not eating, or inappropriate urination).

Cats are also territorial. They don't like to vacate their home turfs, and in strange new places, they feel insecure and stressed by new sounds, smells, and the quest to find safety zones.

You mention that Misha is a bit high-strung. Since moving takes a toll on all members of the household, you will be feeling the stress as well, and she will be detecting your signs of tension. If you are uptight, then she may surmise that something is terribly wrong.

Fortunately, you can do a lot to prepare Misha for your move and the new apartment. The most important step is to introduce her to feeling safe inside a carrier long before moving day. Start by leaving the carrier where Misha likes to catnap. Make it tempting by placing a comfy blanket inside and leaving the door open. Sprinkle some catnip inside if she likes the scent. You are creating good associations with the carrier.

Once Misha seems comfortable in the carrier, shut her in it and take her out to your car. Just hang out with her for a few minutes without turning on the ignition. Gradually work up to taking her on short car rides.

As moving day approaches, try to stick to as regular a routine as possible. Strange as it sounds, tell Misha about the move and what is happening. Use an upbeat, positive tone. True, she won't know your words, but she will read your mood and posture. Let her sniff and explore packing boxes, tape, and other moving supplies.

I recommend that both you and Misha take a calming herbal blend called Rescue Remedy. This over-the-counter blend of essential botanical oils is available at pet supply stores and health stores. It is not toxic or addictive. Place a dropperful in a glass of water for you and rub a few drops in the tip of Misha's ears (it enters her body through the tiny capillaries in the ears). Some cats may require a calming prescriptive medicine — check with your veterinarian.

If possible, mail a T-shirt that you have worn but not washed to the new location. Yes, this is a strange request, but realtors are used to expecting anything. Request that the realtor or landlord rub the shirt across the baseboards of your new apartment to provide a déjà vu scent to your soon-to-arrive Misha.

During moving day, keep Misha in her carrier in an emptied room and post a big sign alerting the movers not to open this door, because there is a cat inside. You might consider having her spend that day at a cat-friendly boarding facility or at a friend's house where she can have a room to herself.

As you settle into your new place, keep Misha confined in one room with all her amenities (food and water bowls, litter box, bedding, toys). Leave her carrier with her so she can hide in it if she wants. Maybe play a little music to muffle the sounds of unpacking. Let her become comfortable exploring this room for a day or so before you introduce her to other rooms in the apartment.

These strategies help all cats, including high-strung ones like Misha, feel right at home in their new places. Good luck!

# Masters of the Ring

**FELINE AGILITY**, the Cat Fanciers' Association's newest and most fascinating activity, has taken off in the United States, Japan, and Europe. While similar in concept to dog agility, there are some distinct differences. When the cat enters the ring with the handler, he is given time to investigate the surroundings and equipment. When his tail goes up, it is the sign he is ready. The ringmaster starts the clock as the handler encourages the cat with a wand, toy, or laser beam to climb stairs and catwalks, to run through hoops and tunnels, and to weave poles as fast as possible.

Pedigreed cats, random-bred household pets, and cats adopted from shelters are all welcome. Watching how cats react to agility has provided unexpected insights into behavioral differences and breed traits.

For example, Abyssinians, a highly active and responsive breed, are "naturals" in the agility arena. They follow the teaser and are capable of running fast, but often lose time because they are too aware. An Aby will stop to look at someone in the audience.

Japanese Bobtails rank as another of the top agility breeds. At a recent show held at Madison Square Garden in New York City, a six-month-old Bobtail ran the course in 17 seconds. This active breed tends to be extremely responsive to the teaser but can become bored. Exhibitors have learned to skip the allowed practice session and go right into competition.

Among the best competitors are Turkish Vans. These powerful, large, longhaired cats are disciplined and they don't miss an obstacle. Maine Coons will finish the course but tend to be slow. They are a thinking breed and sometimes pause, perhaps to wonder what might be in the tunnel before they enter.

Siamese and the Oriental breeds are easily distracted. They react to the teaser and can run fast, but may wander off and sit. They are simply not motivated to finish anything in a particular hurry. Cornish Rex cats also tend to be flighty and inconsistent but can be fast when they choose to be.

Persian kittens are amusing to watch in the agility ring. Typically unafraid and rarely distracted, they concentrate intently on the lure, go through the tunnel, and jump over hurdles. Adult Persians, though, are not as fast as other breeds. They may pose at the top of the stairs, allowing all to see their beauty.

*Contributed by Joan Miller, all-breed judge*

**FELINE FIRST MATES**

Cats can make ideal companions for those who live on boats. The best seafaring cats have short hair (easier to keep clean in the salt air) and claws (to be able to climb up a rope ladder in case of falling off the boat). They need to be comfortable traveling in carriers and have easy-going personalities. They also need to be leash trained and to readily accept wearing a harness.

# On the Road

**Q** My husband is completing his medical internship in Boston. When he finishes, we plan to travel by car across the country to live in Seattle. I'm worried about how my cat, Lucy, will handle the long ride. She loves to chat and demands our attention when we're home. She has ridden in the car inside her carrier to the veterinary clinic and other local trips. Sometimes she meows and other times she is quiet. The thought of spending so many days in a car with Lucy makes me nervous, but we want to see a bit of the country. Any advice?

**A** A cross-country road trip with a cat will definitely test your patience. If all goes well, however, Lucy could become the poster cat for AAA by the time you reach Seattle.

I know what you are going through, having transported two cats by car from south Florida to eastern Pennsylvania several years ago. Little Guy and Callie rode in separate carriers in the back, with each carrier secured in place with a seat belt. Callie acted like a feline mime, but Little Guy began the journey howling like a singer trying to set a world's record for belting out tunes. My ears! By day two, I wised up and gave Little Guy some Rescue Remedy, a natural blend of essential oils that calmed him down to the point that he only released sporadic mews for the rest of the ride.

Let's look at this trip from Lucy's point of view. A car ride is full of scary or unfamiliar sounds like honking, hissing from the air conditioner or heater, and a blaring stereo. Cooped up inside a carrier, which is the safest way to ride, she has no clue whether she is coming or going — she can't look out the window, and she certainly doesn't know how to read a road map. The vibration from the road and the swaying of the vehicle is unsettling and might even make her ill. At night, she'll be carted into yet another unfamiliar hotel room and expected to settle down and go to sleep.

Then there is the issue of bathroom breaks. I fitted each of my cat carriers with a mini litter box. They relied on their balance and agility to use them, even at 65 miles per hour or on a curvy road.

It's good that Lucy has made some trips with you in which the final destination was not the veterinary clinic. She needs to develop some positive associations with being placed in a carrier inside your car. I encourage you to continue taking these fun getaway trips with her to build up her "mileage" of enjoyable travels.

Please do not be tempted to coddle Lucy by taking her out of her carrier and letting her sit on your lap during the trip. The best place for a cat to ride in a moving vehicle is inside a carrier. When cats become scared, their first thought is to seek a place to hide — like underneath the brake pedal or car seats. That spells d-a-n-g-e-r!

Don't be too alarmed if Lucy doesn't eliminate or eat until you reach your hotel each night. Once she calms down from the ride, she will be more inclined to use the litter box, eat, and drink.

Do not leave Lucy in the car when you go to dine at a sit-down restaurant, especially during extremely hot or cold weather. It takes only a few minutes for a cat to become sick, even die, from heat stroke. Seek out places that will allow you to bring her along inside her carrier, such as outdoor cafes.

Be sure to give Lucy lots of therapeutic massages and cuddles each night at your hotel. These will help convey to her that even though she is on the road, she is traveling with two people who love her and make her feel safe.

If your cat has a tendency to become sick and vomit when in the car, consult your veterinarian about appropriate anti-nausea medication that could make the trip easier on both of you.

## TRAVELING CAT CHECKLIST

Before you hit the road with your cat, stock your car with the following supplies:

- ◆ A well-ventilated cat carrier with an easy-to-clean floor pad
- ◆ Bottled water and a no-spill bowl
- ◆ Dry food, small bowl, and treats
- ◆ Favorite toys
- ◆ Comfy, familiar blanket
- ◆ A leash and a spare collar and ID tags with a reachable phone number
- ◆ Cat first-aid kit
- ◆ Travel litter box, litter, and cleaning supplies
- ◆ Nonprescription calming medicine such as Rescue Remedy
- ◆ Photo of your cat in case she gets lost
- ◆ Medical records of your cat
- ◆ Paper towel rolls and plastic bags

# To Board or Not to Board

**Q** We're planning a three-week European vacation next summer with my entire family, including my parents, my husband, and our children. We all are excited about this trip, but we are debating whether to board our two cats or to hire a pet sitter to take care of them. With all of us traveling together, we don't have our normal cat sitters. Either option is expensive, but we don't want to worry about them when we're gone. Bonnie and Clyde are siblings, about four years old, who are very bonded with each other. They are basically indoor cats and have traveled with us for weekend visits at my parents' home without much fuss. Which option would work out best for them?

**A** You won't find many cats packing passports. Home is where the feline heart is. If they were people, some cats would be labeled agoraphobic. Because your cats would probably choose to stay home, the pet-sitting option is definitely worth considering. The main benefit of pet sitting is that Bonnie and Clyde are able to stay put with all their "creature comforts." Even though your absence will upset their normal routine, they will be surrounded by familiar scents and will be comforted by being on their own turf.

Like pet resorts, pet sitting is a booming industry. I recommend interviewing professional sitters who are licensed and bonded and belong to a national organization such as Pet Sitters International or the National Association of Professional Pet Sitters. Pet sitters are trained to feed your cat, administer medications, and scoop the litter boxes. They also are available to water your plants, make sure your windows and doors are locked, take in the newspaper and mail, and even take out the trash.

The downside is that pet sitters tend to be busy people. They typically make one or two visits a day to your home. If a medical problem or other mishap should happen to Bonnie or Clyde, it might be 24 hours before someone could respond.

If you are fortunate enough to have a trusted friend, relative, or neighbor who is willing to step in and kitty-sit, this is also an option. I am less keen about hiring college students or others who are not professionally trained as pet sitters. Their motivation is money, and they may not put your cats' needs as a priority, not out of meanness but from not knowing feline needs. Always provide a written list of instructions on how to care for your cats and what to do in case of a medical emergency.

**FELINE FACT**
Cats purr at the frequency of 25 vibrations per second.

Now let's consider the boarding option. In addition to the traditional veterinary clinic boarding, there is an increasing array of specialty kennels that cater to your pet's every whim. Instead of going to the dogs, these places are going to the cats. Some places look like mini-condos, complete with a television set, piped-in music, plush bedding, two levels, window perches, and other cat amenities. At last count, there were more than 9,000 boarding kennels in North America, and that number is rapidly growing as more folks are traveling — and as more people are willing to spend serious money on fancy boarding facilities for their pets.

If you decide to board Bonnie and Clyde, look for cat-only kennels, especially if your cats have not had a lot of whisker-to-whisker time with dogs. A feline environment will be more soothing to your cats, without all that barking, whining, and howling. It's important that you visit the places before booking, rather than relying on ads or information collected over the phone from the kennel staff.

When you visit, pay attention to how the staff interact with their feline guests. You definitely want "cat people"

who will cuddle and call your cats by their names. Ask what the ratio of staff to cats is, if the place is staffed 24 hours a day, and if there is a veterinarian on call to handle medical emergencies. The kennel should be clean, and you should not detect any odors. Take a careful look at the feline guests and determine if they look content or act edgy or scared. And don't forget to arrange for Bonnie and Clyde to share a run. Since they are close companions, staying together will help ease the distress of being away from home.

Since your trip won't occur for several months, I encourage you to take a test run by booking Bonnie and Clyde for a night or two at a kennel. If they appear totally stressed out when you pick them up, that's a sign that the kennel life, even at a fancy feline resort, is not for them.

So, what's my vote? That's a tough call. Try the boarding for a couple of days, wait a week or so, and then the next time you plan to see your folks for a weekend, leave Bonnie and Clyde with a pet sitter and see how they do. You should be able to tell from their behavior which option makes the most sense for your duo. With names like Bonnie and Clyde, you want to keep them happy!

**FELINE FACT**
Puss reigns as the Methuselah of felines. This British cat died in 1939 at the grand old age of 36.

# A CAT'S AGE IN HUMAN YEARS

Figuring out your feline's age can be a frustrating exercise. The myth of "one cat year equals seven human years" is just that — a myth. Cats reach senior status by the age of 7 and are considered geriatric by the age of 12.

While there is no reliable scientific method for converting your cat's age into human years, experts report that a 1-year-old cat is roughly equal to a 15-year-old person. The following chart gives you an idea of your cat's age in people years.

| Age of Cat | Comparable Human Age | Age of Cat | Comparable Human Age |
|:---:|:---:|:---:|:---:|
| 1 | 15 | 12 | 64 |
| 2 | 24 | 13 | 68 |
| 3 | 28 | 14 | 72 |
| 4 | 32 | 15 | 76 |
| 5 | 36 | 16 | 80 |
| 6 | 40 | 17 | 84 |
| 7 | 44 | 18 | 88 |
| 8 | 48 | 19 | 92 |
| 9 | 52 | 20 | 96 |
| 10 | 56 | 21 | 100 |
| 11 | 60 | | |

## PROFESSIONAL CONSULTANTS

**ALICE MOON-FANELLI** is a certified applied animal behaviorist and clinical assistant professor at Cummings School of Veterinary Medicine at Tufts University, North Grafton, MA. She works in the Animal Behavior Center, which offers a remote consultation service (www.tufts.edu/vet/petfax). She received her doctorate and master's degrees in etiology and canine behavior genetics from the University of Connecticut. An expert on cat, dog, and wolf behavior, Dr. Moon-Fanelli is a regular contributor to *Catnip* and *Your Dog* magazines.

**JOAN MILLER** is an all-breed judge and legislative coordinator of the Cat Fanciers' Association, the world's largest registry of pedigreed cats. A breeder of cats for more than two decades, she is considered one of the world's top authorities on the history, genetic makeup, and personality traits of the various feline breeds. She is former president of the Winn-Feline Foundation, a nonprofit group that awards grants for feline research. She lives in San Diego. To learn more about CFA, please visit their Web site: www.cfainc.org.

**ARNOLD PLOTNICK** is board-certified by both the American College of Veterinary Internal Medicine and the American Board of Veterinary Practitioners. One of a handful of board-certified cat specialists in the United States, Dr. Plotnick operates a cats-only practice called the Manhattan Cat Specialists in New York City (www.manhattancats.com). He is the medical editor of *Catnip* magazine, writes a monthly medical column for *Cat Fancy* magazine, serves on the editorial advisory board of Veterinary Forum, and provides advice on CatChannel.com. He earned his doctorate in veterinary medicine from the University of Florida in Gainesville.

## SELECTED RESOURCES

Alley Cat Allies, *www.alleycat.org*

American Society for the Prevention of Cruelty to Animals, *www.aspca.org*

Animal Humane Association, *www.americanhumane.org*

Cat Fanciers' Association, *www.cfainc.org*

Cornell Feline Health Center, *www.vet.cornell.edu/fhc*

Delta Society, *www.deltasociety.org*

Humane Society of the United States, *www.hsus.org*

The International Cat Association, *www.tica.org*

Morris Animal Foundation, *www.morrisanimalfoundation.org*

PetDiets.com, *www.petdiets.com*

## ANIMAL BEHAVIOR

Animal Behavior Network, *www.animalbehavior.net*

International Association of Animal Behavior Consultants, *www.iaabc.org*

Winn-Feline Foundation, *www.winnfelinehealth.com*

Animal Behavior Clinic at Cummings School of Veterinary Medicine at Tufts University, *www.tufts.edu/vet/petfax*

## LIVING WITH PETS

Dating Web sites for people with pets.
*www.animalattraction.com*
*www.animalpeople.com*
*www.datemypet.com*

Sites to help you find pet-friendly housing.
*www.apartmentguide.com*
*www.forrent.com*
*www.rentwithpets.com*

Seek pet sitters in your area.
*www.petsitter.org*
*www.petsit.com*

## LOSS OF A PET

Organizations that can help you deal with the death of a pet.

Association for Pet Loss & Bereavement, *www.aplb.org*

Rainbow Bridge, *www.rainbowbridge.com*

Tufts University Pet Loss Support Hotline
508-839-7966
*www.tufts.edu/vet/petloss/*

University of California-Davis, School of Veterinary Medicine
Pet Loss Support Hotline
800-565-1526
*www.vetmed.ucdavis.edu/petloss/index.htm*

## RECOMMENDED READING

Adams, Janine. *How to Say It to Your Cat.* Prentice Hall Press, 2003.

Ballner, Maryjean. *Cat Massage.* St. Martin's Griffin, 1997.

Beck, Alan. *Between Pets and People: The Importance of Animal Companionship.* Purdue University Press, 1996.

Becker, Marty. *The Healing Power of Pets.* Hyperion, 2002.

Dodman, Nicholas. *The Cat Who Cried for Help.* Bantam Books, 1997.

Johnson-Bennett, Pam. *Think Like a Cat.* Penguin Books, 2000.

Landsberg, Gary, Wayne Hunthausen, and Lowell Ackerman. *Handbook of Behavior Problems of the Dog and Cat.* Elsevier Saunders, 2003.

Moore, Arden. *The Kitten Owner's Manual.* Storey Publishing, 2001.

———. *50 Simple Ways to Pamper Your Cat.* Storey Publishing, 2000.

Rainbolt, Dusty. *Kittens for Dummies.* For Dummies, 2003.

Shojai, Amy. *PETiquette: Solving Behavior Problems in Your Multi-Pet Household.* M. Evans and Company, Inc., 2005.

Walker, Bob. *The Cats' House.* Andrews and McMeel, 1996.

Wright, John C. *Is Your Cat Crazy?* Hungry Minds, 1996.

## INDEX

Page numbers in **bold** indicate tables.